Sip 'n SEW

By Diane Dhein

©2008 by Diane Dhein
Published by

 krause publications
An Imprint of F+W Publications

700 East State Street • Iola, WI 54990-0001
715-445-2214 • 888-457-2873
www.krausebooks.com

Our toll-free number to place an order or obtain a free catalog is (800) 258-0929.

The following trademarked terms and companies appear in this publication:

50/50™, 7UP®, Aleene's® Thick Designer Tacky Glue™, Amazing Designs®, Baby Lock® Embellisher, Country Time® Raspberry Lemonade, Designer's Gallery®, LetterWorks™, Designer's Gallery® MasterWorks™, E-Z Load® Memory Book, Fasturn® Set. Fray Check™, Gingher®, HeatnBond®, Hydro-stick™ Tear-away, Insul-Bright™, Kool-Aid®, Libbey®, Lipton®, Luzianne®, Nestle® Coffee-mate®, Olfa®, Omnigrid®, Oster®, Pellon® ShirTailor®, Pellon® Thermolam® Plus, Pellon® Wonder-Under®, Sewing With Nancy® Fab Felter™, Splenda®, Sprite® Squirt®, Steam-A-Seam 2®, Sulky® KK2000™, Sulky® Sliver Metallic thread, Sulky® Ultra Solvy™, Sunkist®, Tang®, Teflon®, Velcro®, Warm & Natural® batting, Welch's®, and WoolFelt®.

Library of Congress Control Number: 2007939099

ISBN 13: 978-0-89689-552-2
ISBN 10: 0-89689-552-1

Designed by Rachael Knier
Edited by Erica Swanson

Printed in China

Acknowledgments

The fortitude for writing a book lies within yourself; it is prompted by those people around you who care about you and believe in your creativity. There are several people I would like to thank for giving me encouragement:

My husband, Lynn, who was very supportive in my endeavor. It was his reassurance that helped me through this past year of writing and creating projects. He also learned to cook with expertise and to clean with gusto!

My daughter, Angie, who gave me artful inspiration. My son, Mitch, and daughter, Lara, along with other family and friends, also continually supported my writing efforts. They especially encouraged me to test all of the beverages on them!

My patient editor, Erica Swanson, acquisitions editor, Candy Wiza, and designer, Rachael Knier, along with all the wonderful people at Krause Publications who have worked with me. I would also like to thank the photographer, Kris Kandler, and photo stylists, Mary Collette and Lynn Hallmark.

My friend, Laure Noe, who did an awesome job with the illustrations. Pat Hahn was my preliminary proof master and confidante.

Friends and colleagues at Nancy's Notions, who never doubted my abilities. I would especially like to thank my dear friends, Nancy and Phyllis.

Table of Contents

Flavors & Techniques

Introduction

Like many people, I have always enjoyed sewing and cooking for my family. My life has always revolved around the domestic arts, both at home and in my career. My children used to think I was a little tailor who would make clothes for them in the wee hours of the morning, laying them out to greet them in the morning. I also love to concoct new recipes, and I am addicted to collecting cookbooks. I have far more than I could ever actually use in a lifetime!

In this book, I have compiled some of my family's favorite beverage recipes, along with easy gifts for various occasions. The projects are perfect for you, or for someone you know who would enjoy learning a lifelong hobby—and best of all, they can be completed in just a few hours! I hope you will enjoy making them as much as I did creating them.

Sip as you sew, if you like. Some of the recipes probably should be enjoyed AFTER you have completed the project. But after all, the "sewing police" won't arrest you if you can't sew a straight line!

Have fun making the recipes and projects featured in this book. Take some time out of your busy life, and relax with a mug and a project.

Foreword

Diane has been my friend and co-worker for over 20 years. As a member of the Sewing With Nancy team, she's the go-to person when we need a tasteful, yet easy-to-sew project. She's also the person who on potluck or treat days always, I mean always, brings tastefully prepared and beautifully presented dishes to pass. (No box-cake mixes in Diane's kitchen.) You might say, Diane brings good taste to both sewing and cooking.

Nancy Zieman

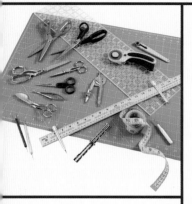

Chapter 1: Getting Started

Work up a thirst, because you'll love making the beverage recipes in this book to quench it! There are recipes to sip for just about every mood and holiday throughout the year! Sew while you sip and create quick and crafty projects suitable for gifts or for your own home décor. Most of the recipes and projects are designed to utilize basic equipment. However, specialty items are featured with individual projects to make your job easier.

Sewing Equipment and Techniques

If you have a notion to create, you'll need some supplies! There are many gadgets on the market, and these are some of my favorite basics.

Measuring and Cutting

The elementary 6" gauge is an essential notion for sewing. It is usually marked in inches and centimeters, and it is great for small measurements. A tape measure comes in handy when you need to measure around curved items. A 6" x 24" clear ruler is the most popular size ruler. It is not only used to measure, but also as a straight edge guide when using a rotary cutter. A yardstick is needed for the yardstick compass when making a large circle up to 72" in diameter, while a regular school-type compass is sufficient for smaller circles.

Keep a small sharp scissors at your sewing machine for trimming threads and clipping as you sew. Use high-quality shears for cutting out patterns and cutting through several layers. A scissors has two smaller holes while a shears has one small hole for your thumb and one large hole for fingers.

Rotary cutters have a rolling blade similar to a pizza cutter. Using a rotary cutter is a very efficient way to cut fabric, especially strips. There are a variety of shapes and sizes. The 45 mm. rotary cutter is a favorite, and an ergonomic handle is highly recommended. Be careful when using rotary cutters, because they are sharp enough to slice through up to eight layers of fabric. Save old blades if you have more than one cutter, because they are still sharp enough to cut paper and cardboard. Make sure to mark the cutter used for paper with a permanent marker.

A cutting mat and ruler are necessary when using a rotary cutter. There are many sizes of cutting mats, but the 18" x 24" mat marked with 1" grid lines is the most popular.

A pinking shears is decorative as well as functional. Use it to trim around curves, to clean finish seam edges, or as a decorative trimmer. Use scalloping shears for a decoratively finished edge.

Pinning and Marking

Choose pins that work well for you—there is no set rule. Flat-head pins work well if you need to place a ruler over your project to trim, because they won't throw your cutting out of balance. They are also easy to pick up and to find when dropped. Glass-head pins are great for projects that require a lot of pressing, because if you touch a glass-head pin with your iron, you won't melt the head. When you need to do a lot of

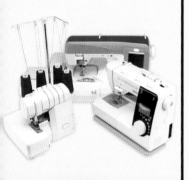

pinning, curved basting pins are easy to use. You are also less likely to stick yourself with them, as the pin point is not as exposed as on regular safety pins.

Water-soluble markers and chalk markers are easy to see and can be spritzed or washed away. Always remove markings made with water-soluble markers before pressing the fabric, because pressing can set those markings. Permanent fabric markers are especially helpful for adding detail to fabric projects and signing the back of your projects because the ink will not bleed when washed.

Sewing Machines, Embroidery Machines, and Sergers

A simple sewing machine is all that you need for most of the projects in this book. Purchase the best quality machine you can afford, keep it maintained, and take any lessons that are offered with it. Embroidery on the projects is optional. A serger is suggested for a few of the projects, but it is also optional.

Thread and Needles

Use all-purpose 100% polyester thread for most of the projects in this book. Choose cotton thread for projects made of all-cotton fabric, and select a heavier 12 wt. cotton thread for decorative serging. To eliminate thread changes on multicolored projects, use clear monofilament thread. Rayon thread adds sheen and luster for the optional embroidery.

Choose universal size 80/12 needles for most sewing. Additional needles, such as denim sharps for denim, embroidery for machine embroidery, and Microtex for synthetic suede may also be helpful.

An assortment of hand-sewing needles for general sewing and chenille needles for embroidery are practical to have on hand.

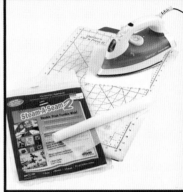

Fusing and Pressing

There are many paper-backed fusibles on the market. Most of the projects that use fusibles in this book suggest a no-sew paper-backed fusible. This type seals the edges of the fabric so that it doesn't ravel. Some no-sew paper-backed fusibles are designed so you also can sew through them. That's an advantage if you would like to sew on trim or decide to appliqué on it. Then you won't have problems with your needle gumming up.

A high-quality iron that can be used on either a steam or dry setting and a pressing surface are necessities for sewing and craft projects. A cotton press cloth is a nice addition to your pressing area, as well as a non-stick appliqué pressing sheet.

Gluing

A thick fabric glue and a small brush (to apply it) are a must for small craft projects. A glue gun and glue sticks are another option for many craft projects. Use the type of glue suggested in the project supply list.

Temporary spray adhesive is recommended for many projects. There are many different spray adhesives on the market. Choose one that sprays evenly, doesn't clump, and won't turn your fabric yellow. Suggestions are given with projects in which they are recommended.

Enlarging Patterns

Many of the patterns for projects on the following pages were too large to fit on the pages. They are scaled to size with each square representing ¼". Draw them on ¼" graph paper to enlarge them. Graph paper is available at office supply stores and many large chain stores. The projects are worth the extra effort.

Enlarge patterns using graph paper.

Each pattern includes the percentage for enlargement if you decide to have your local copy shop enlarge them. Compare measurements to those given in the project copy.

Felting

The felting process has been around for years, but the Felting Mat and Tool make it so easy to do! For an even quicker felting method, there are felting machines available such as the Sewing With Nancy Fab Felter and the Baby Lock Embellisher. These machines are especially helpful if you have large areas that you wish to felt.

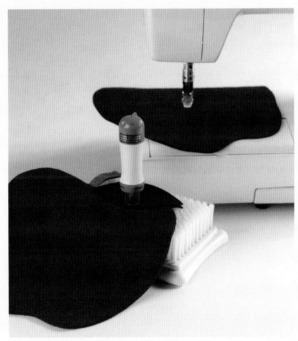

Felting machine, felting mat, and tool.

Binding

Everyone has a favorite binding technique. The following method is simple, and the one I use most often:

1. Measure the edge that is going to be bound and add 1" for each corner and 3"–4" for an overlap. Cut the number of crosswise strips needed to accommodate this measurement. (Example: If you need 67" of binding, you'll need to cut two 42" crosswise strips. Trim off the excess as you join the ends of the binding.)

2. Join strips together by stitching the short ends, right sides together, with diagonal seams.

3. Trim the beginning end of the strip at a 45-degree angle and turn under ¼" to clean finish that end. Use a ¼"-wide strip of paper-backed fusible web to secure the finished edge and make it easier to use.

Trim the strip at an angle, turn under ¼", and attach paper-backed fusible web.

4. Mark the project ¼" from each corner with a pin.

Corners marked with pins.

5. Press the binding in half length-wise, wrong sides together, and stitch it to the project using a ¼" seam, starting about 3"–4" from the end of the strip.

Stitching binding.

6. When you reach a pin, take a couple stitches in place. Clip threads.

7. Fold binding up and then back over corner to allow for miter. Begin stitching at the fold of the binding.

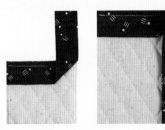

Fold binding to form corner miter.

8. Repeat this technique at each corner.

9. Trim excess fabric from end of binding, allowing enough fabric to insert into the starting end of the binding. Continue stitching.

10. Fold the binding to the wrong side of your project, covering the stitching line. Tuck in the corners of the binding to form miters.

11. Hand stitch the binding from the wrong side of your project.

Hand stitch the binding in place.

Now that you are familiar with the basic equipment and a few techniques, you are ready to Sip 'n Sew!

Chapter 2:
Teatime Treasures

You can span the world looking for recipes that are right under your teacup. Create specialty teas and projects that are fun and festive. Make gifts that are heartfelt and appeal to southern charm, or accessorize a tea party with an atmosphere of good karma.

SCARLETT'S FLORAL TEA COZY

FINISHED SIZE: WILL FIT A 16–24 OUNCE TEAPOT

This tea cozy is perfect for keeping a pot of Southern Almond Sweet Tea hot. Simply pour the tea in the pot, place the pot in the cozy, and cinch the top shut. Because the spout and handle are exposed, you can pour another cup of tea without removing the cozy. The insulated batting is the key to keeping your teapot cozy and warm.

Supplies:

⅓ yd. cotton Fabric A (outside)

⅓ yd. cotton Fabric B (lining)

⅓ yd. needle punched insulated batting*

1½ yd. 1"–2" lace

1 pkg. coordinating wide single-fold bias tape (or 1⅜"-wide strips of bias to match inside lining fabric)

1 pkg. coordinating single-fold bias tape (⅞"-wide bias strip, before folding)

1 yd. ¼" ribbon

1 spool matching all-purpose thread or monofilament thread

1 small safety pin

Compass

Temporary adhesive basting spray*

Pinking shears (optional)

Walking foot (optional)

Quilting guide (optional)

*I prefer Insul-Bright batting and Sulky KK2000 adhesive.

Instructions:

Note: All seam allowances are ¼" unless otherwise noted.

1. Prepare patterns.

   • Enlarge the Tea Cozy Top pattern piece on page 24, following the instructions on page 12. Transfer the pattern markings.

   • Draw a 7¼" circle for the Tea Cozy Bottom using a compass.

   • Fold the circle in half, and mark the edges at the fold line.

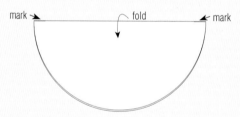

mark ➤   ◠ fold   ◄ mark

2. Cut the fabrics for tea cozy, making sure to transfer the markings.

   • From Fabric A (outside), cut one 11" x 42" strip.

   • From Fabric B (lining), cut one 11" x 42" strip.

   • From the insulated batting, cut one 11" x 42" strip.

3. Layer the fabrics. Lightly spray temporary adhesive basting spray between each layer to eliminate the need for pins.

   • Place Fabric B wrong-side up. Center the insulated batting over Fabric B.

   • Center Fabric A over the insulated batting, right-side up.

4. Quilt the fabrics together.

   • Use a water-soluble fabric marker or chalk to mark diagonal quilting lines ¾" apart on Fabric A. Or, attach a quilting guide to your presser foot.

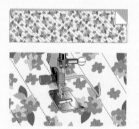

   • Thread your machine with matching all-purpose thread or monofilament thread. Quilt the layers together, stitching along the marked lines. Use a walking foot, if desired.

The gripper teeth on the bottom of a walking foot help feed the top layer of fabric evenly as the sewing machine's feed dogs feed the bottom layer. Start quilting from the center, and work out to each side.

5. Place the pattern pieces on the quilted fabric and cut two Tea Cozy Tops and one Tea Cozy Bottom circle. Transfer markings to Tea Cozy Tops and Bottom.

6. Sew lace and binding to each of the Tea Cozy tops.

   • Press the wide single-fold bias open; then fold in half lengthwise.

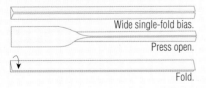

Wide single-fold bias.

Press open.

Fold.

• Place lace wrong-side up on the right side of the Tea Cozy Top, starting at the bottom edge. Place folded bias on top of the lace, with all raw edges even.

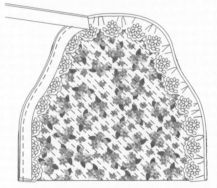

Stitch binding over lace.

• Stitch through all layers ¼" from the edge, attaching lace and bias around the upper edges of the cozy. Trim the insulated batting close to the stitching.

NOTABLE

Cut the layered fabric into thirds (approximately 11" x 14" each) to make quilting easier.

• Turn the bias to the reverse side of the tea cozy, covering the original stitching line, and topstitch in place. Topstitching will show on the right side, and binding will show on the reverse side.

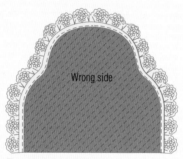

Topstitch binding.

• For the cozy front, separate two pieces of bias. Fold under the bias ends in the middle and side edges on the cozy front. Trim excess bias. Stitch bias tape on both sides along the placement line at the top of the cozy.

7. Add the cinch.

• For the cozy back, stitch single-fold bias tape on both sides along the line marked at the top of the cozy. Tuck bias ends under at the side edges. Trim excess bias. Pin. Stitch.

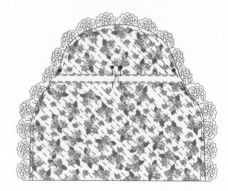

8. Complete the tea cozy.

- Match the bottom of the front tea cozy with the half marks on the circular bottom, right sides together. Pin in place. Stitch.

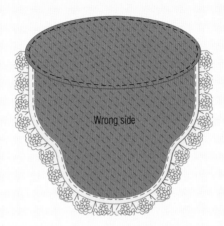

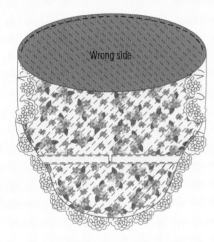

- Add the back tea cozy bottom, butting bias ends together and overlapping lace. Stitch remaining ¼" seam.

- Trim excess batting from seam. Trim seam with a pinking shears, if desired. Turn the tea cozy right-side out.

- Use a bodkin or safety pin to thread the ¼" ribbon into the bias casing, starting and ending at the front middle section of the cozy.

9. Place a teapot in the cozy and cinch the top shut, tying the ribbon into a bow. Now your teapot will stay warm and toasty!

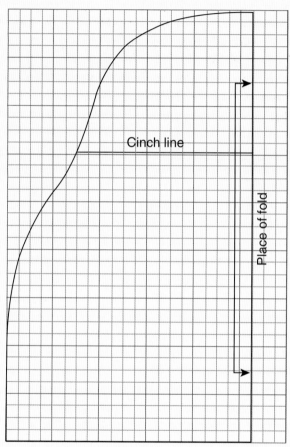

Cinch line

Place of fold

Tea Cozy Top—Enlarge 200%

SOUTHERN ALMOND SWEET TEA
6–8 SERVINGS

Sweet tea is a staple beverage of the south. Sugar or another sweetener is mixed with hot water to make a thick, syrupy concentrate before it is added to the tea mixture. The juice and extracts used in this recipe infuse the tea with a flavor Miss Scarlett would savor!

Ingredients:

3 regular tea bags*

6 cups cold water

1 cup sugar (or equivalent sweetener)

⅔ cup lemon juice (3–4 fresh-squeezed lemons)

1 ½ tsp. pure almond extract

1 tsp. pure vanilla extract

Amaretto liqueur to taste (optional)

*I prefer Luzianne or Lipton tea.

Directions:

1. Bring 2 cups water to a boil. Add three tea bags. Remove from heat and let steep for about 10 minutes. Remove tea bags.

2. In a separate pan, bring 4 cups of water to a boil and add sugar. Let the sugar mixture simmer for 5 minutes; then add fresh lemon juice, almond and vanilla extracts.

3. Combine the sugar mixture with the tea. Add Amaretto, if desired.

4. Serve tea hot or iced. Garnish with a lemon twist. Add a sprig of mint for a more "high-falutin' drink!"

NOTABLE

To increase the amount of juice you can get from a lemon, microwave the whole lemon on high power for 20–30 seconds before cutting and squeezing it.

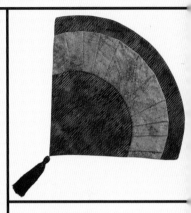

ASIAN TEA PARTY MAT

FINISHED SIZE: 10½" X 12½"

A fan-shaped tea mat is ideal for a perfect "chi" party! Serve a special tea or dessert on this fanciful little mat. It has to be good karma!

Supplies (for two mats):

⅓ yd. muslin

⅓ yd. Fabric A (mat topper, bottom, and back)

½ yd. Fabric B (mat center band)

Two 8½" x 11" sheets paper-backed fusible web*

*I prefer Steam-A-Seam 2.

Instructions:

1. Enlarge the Tea Party Mat pattern on page 156, following the instructions on page 12. Trace and cut out one complete mat, one mat bottom, and one mat topper on paper. Trace all cutting and placement markings onto the patterns.

2. Cut your fabric.

 • Cut two complete fan-shaped mats from muslin. Transfer markings to both sides of the muslin mats.

 • From Fabric A, cut two mat bottoms and two complete mats backs.

 • With Fabric B (center band), fold one end of 18" fabric on the bias. Trim along the cut edge on the fabric and along the fold, forming two triangles (one for each mat).

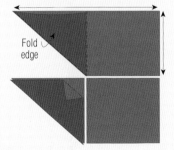

Fold edge

NOTABLE

Steam-A-Seam 2 has paper on both sides. To find the correct side for tracing the pattern, gently peel the layers apart at a corner. Trace the pattern on the side to which the web sticks.

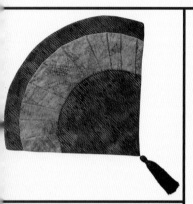

3. Prepare the mat topper appliqué.

- Trace two of mat topper pattern on paper-backed fusible web.

- Roughly cut out mat toppers about ¼" from the traced edge.

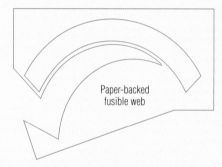

Paper-backed fusible web

- Remove the paper backing from the wrong side of the fusible web, exposing the fusible web.

- Press the paper-backed fusible web patterns to the wrong side of Fabric A. Cut the mat toppers, following traced lines.

- Remove paper backing and press the appliqué into position on the muslin fan. Repeat for the second fan.

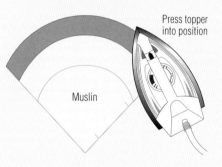

Press topper into position

Muslin

4. Shape the pleated center band.

- Center one of the appliquéd muslin fabric fans on the long edge of a Fabric B triangle, with right sides together. The lower edge of the mat topper should be about ¼" from the bottom edge of the fabric.

- Stitch ¼" from placement line for mat topper on wrong side of muslin.

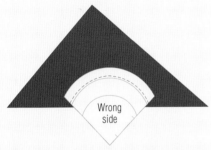

Stitch ¼" up from placement line #1.

- Turn the mat to the right side, and fold down the fabric triangle in gentle folds, smoothing the seam line. Press gently.

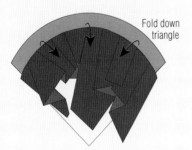

Fold down triangle

5. Complete the fan-shaped mats.

- Stitch ¼" from the top curved edge of the fan bottom. Turn the top edge to the wrong side along the stitching line. Press. Repeat steps 4 and 5 for the second fan.

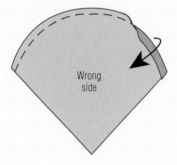

Wrong side

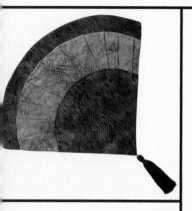

• Pin the fan bottom into position over the pleated center band. Topstitch in place. Repeat for the second fan.

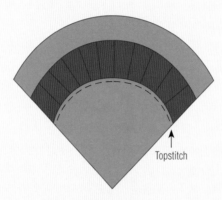

Topstitch

• Lift the fan bottoms, and trim excess fabric from the center band as necessary.

• Center the mat back over the mat front, right sides together. Stitch around the mat, leaving an opening between the side markings for turning. Reinforce the point by stitching twice. Repeat for the second mat.

• Trim the seam, clip the point, and pink the curved fan edge. Turn right-side out. Repeat for the second mat.

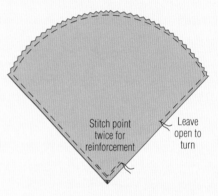

Stitch point twice for reinforcement

Leave open to turn

• Stitch the opening closed by hand with small concealed stitches. Repeat for the second mat.

Create your own good fortune! Serve Mandarin Spice Tea in an artisan-inspired teacup on an Asian Tea Party Mat.

TRUFFLE TAKE-OUT BOX

FINISHED SIZE: 1¾" X 2⅛" X 1⅝"

Create a unique hostess gift with these mini Truffle Take-out Boxes. They are the perfect size for a fortune cookie, mints, or some gourmet nuts.

Supplies (makes two):

8½" x 11" sheet of poster board or cardstock

9" x 12" rectangle of cotton fabric

8½" x 11" sheet of no-sew paper-backed fusible web*

Embossing tool

Teflon pressing sheet

Ruler

Scissors

Iron

Pencil

Thick, quick-drying glue

*I prefer Steam-A-Seam 2 or HeatnBond Ultra, and Aleene's Thick Designer Tacky Glue.

Instructions:

1. Iron paper-backed fusible web to an 8½" x 11" sheet of card-stock, following manufacturer's instructions.

2. Remove the paper from the back of the cardstock. Meet the fusible web to the wrong side of the fabric, and press with a dry iron.

3. Copy the Truffle Take-out Box pattern on page 157. Cut out.

4. Trace two box patterns on the cardstock side of the fabric, including all dashed lines. Cut out both boxes on the solid lines.

5. Score the dashed lines from the cardstock side of the fabric, using the embossing tool and a ruler.

6. Construct the box by folding and gluing the side tab and then the bottom tabs.

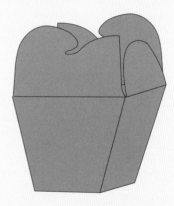

7. Fold in B flaps and then the A flaps, interlocking the A flaps.

MANDARIN SPICE TEA

6–8 SERVINGS

The Mandarin Oranges on a bamboo kabob add a touch of the Orient to this spicy orange tea. Drink it hot or cold—either way, your taste buds are in for a real treat!

Ingredients:

1 tsp. whole cloves

1 stick cinnamon

¼ tsp. orange zest

3 black tea bags

6 cups water

6 oz. orange juice concentrate

½ tsp. lime juice

¼ cup fresh-squeezed lemon juice (1–2 lemons)

½ cup sugar

¼ cup honey

Mandarin orange slices (canned or fresh) for garnish

Directions:

1. Tie spices loosely in cheese-cloth. Place in water and bring to a boil.

2. Add tea bags, turn off heat, and steep for 8 minutes.

3. Remove the tea bags (do not squeeze them).

4. Heat fruit juices, sugar, and honey. Add to the tea.

5. Serve hot or chilled over ice. Garnish with mandarin orange slices on a bamboo kabob stick.

TISSUE COVERLET

This simple project is a palette to feature your favorite embroidery. The coverlet fits a tall tissue box, and it is a perfect gift with orange spice tea for a friend with the sniffles!

Supplies:

½ yd. cotton print Fabric A

9" x 9" Fabric B (cotton fabric for embroidery)

½ yd. polyester fleece batting

2 yd. pre-gathered lace (¾" wide)

1⅛ yd. ⅜" ribbon to match cotton print

Boutique-style tissue box

Embroidery supplies (optional): design of your choice, rayon thread, lightweight bobbin thread, and sticky-back wash-away stabilizer*

*I prefer Wash-Away Extra.

Instructions:

1. Prepare the paper patterns.

   • Cut one 10" x 15" rectangle for the coverlet pattern. Mark one 15" side "top," and mark the opposite end "bottom."

   • Cut one 15" square for lining pattern.

• Cut one 5" square from each bottom corner of coverlet pattern, and cut a 5" square from each corner of lining pattern. Mark top fold lines as illustrated.

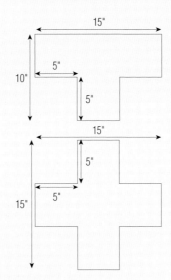

2. Cut Fabrics.

   • From Fabric A, cut one coverlet pattern and one lining pattern.

NOTABLE

The embroidery design used on the Tissue Coverlet is from Sew Precious Creations.

- From Fabric B, cut one end panel 5" wide x 5½" long.

- Cut one piece of batting using the lining pattern.

3. Prepare Fabric B end panel for embroidery (optional).

  - Fold end panel to find center, and mark with crosshairs for embroidery placement.

  - Place sticky back wash-away stabilizer in the embroidery hoop. Peel away the paper inside the hoop, following manufacturer's instructions.

  - Place the end panel on top of the sticky stabilizer, right-side up, matching the crosshairs with the markings on the hoop.

  - Embroider a design of your choice. A design approximately 3¼" wide x 3¾" high is a good size for this project.

  - Remove excess stabilizer. Spritz with water to remove any remaining stabilizer from the project. Press from the reverse side.

4. Attach the embroidered end panel to the coverlet.

  - Center the end panel, right sides together, on the long top edge of the coverlet, with raw edges even. Make sure the embroidery is facing the correct direction.

  - Stitch, using a ¼" seam. Press seam open.

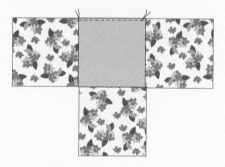

5. Attach lace and ribbon.

  - Place the coverlet over the batting. Pin in place. Stitch along the fold lines at the top of the coverlet.

- Pin lace around all edges of the coverlet, with right sides together and lace facing the inside of the coverlet. Pin a tuck in the lace at each corner to ease in fullness.

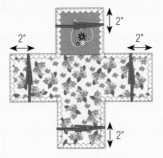

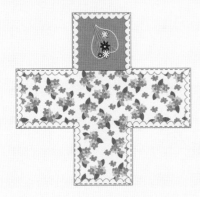

- Machine-baste the lace in place. Trim any excess batting.

- Cut the ribbon into eight 6"–7" pieces, and tack it to the sides of the coverlet about 2" from the side edges of the bottom.

6. Complete the coverlet.

- With right sides together, lay the lining over the coverlet. Pin in place.

- Stitch around the coverlet with a ¼" seam, catching the bottom ends of the ties in the stitching. Leave a 3" opening on one edge for turning.

- Trim excess fabric and batting, clip corners, and turn right-side out. Make a 2½"–3" buttonhole in the top center of the coverlet through all layers.

- Place the coverlet over your tissue box, and tie ribbons to secure.

ORANGE SPICE TEA MIX

36–38 SERVINGS

If you love instant spice tea, this one is a "keeper!" Store the tea in a covered container, ready to mix with water for a relaxing treat. Or, bag it and add a direction card to give a friend who is a little under the weather.

Ingredients:

1 cup unsweetened instant ice tea mix

2 cups orange-flavored breakfast drink*

2 pkgs. (0.23 oz. each) unsweetened lemonade drink mix*

2½ cups sugar

1 tsp. ground cinnamon

1 tsp. ground cloves

½ tsp. ground nutmeg

1 tsp. each of dried lemon and orange zest (optional)

*I prefer Tang breakfast drink and Kool-Aid drink mix.

Directions:

1. Mix all ingredients together. Store in a covered container.

2. Add 2 Tbsp. mix to 8 oz. hot or cold water. Garnish with a slice of lemon or orange.

Photocopy this card on cardstock paper. Attach to your beverage mix.

To serve Orange Spice Tea:

Add 2 Tbsp. mix to 8 oz. hot or cold water. Garnish with a slice of lemon or orange.

Savor the flavor!

NOTABLE

Make lemon or orange zest by using a small grater or zester to scrape the peel from the fruit. Use only the colorful area of the fruit; the peel is bitter as you scrape deeper. Place the zest on wax paper and let it air-dry for several hours or overnight before adding it to the tea mix.

CHAI CUP WALL HANGING

FINISHED SIZE: 9" X 9" (NOT INCLUDING TIES)

A Chai (tea) Cup Wall Hanging is the perfect place to use Auntie's favorite hanky and make a memento with flair. Use the teacup appliqué pattern provided, or choose your favorite embroidery.

Supplies:

⅓ yd. cotton Fabric A (background, binding, and backing)

⅛ yd. cotton Fabric B (teacup)

¼ yd. low-loft batting

8½" x 11" sheet of no-sew paper-backed fusible web*

⅛ yd. medium-weight fusible interfacing

1 small hanky or doily

Matching all-purpose thread

Curved basting pins, size 1

Fine-tip permanent fabric pen (optional)*

Open-toe foot and 8" square tear-away stabilizer for satin stitch appliqué (optional)

4 grommets and 2 yd. each of two ¼" ribbons to match fabric (optional)

*I prefer Steam-A-Seam 2 and a Pigma Pen (size 05).

Instructions:

1. Cut the fabrics.

   • From Fabric A, cut one 2½" crosswise strip for binding and one 9" crosswise strip. Subcut the 9" strip into two 9" squares for the background and backing.

   • Cut one 9" square from batting.

   • Cut one 1" x 9" strip from interfacing.

   • Cut off the tip of hanky on the diagonal, no larger than the measurements in the illustration. Press under ¼" to the wrong side, on the cut edge.

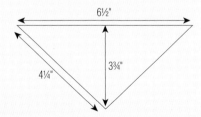

6½"

3¾"

4¼"

2. Prepare the appliqué for the teacup using the pattern on page 154.

- Trace the Teacup pattern on the paper side of the fusible web.

- Roughly cut out the traced appliqué about ¼" from the traced pattern.

- Press the traced appliqué pattern to the wrong side of Fabric B.

- Cut out the appliqué, following the traced lines.

3. Fuse a 1" strip of interfacing to the top edge of the background rectangle, wrong sides together.

4. Position the hanky and Teacup appliqué on the background fabric.

- Measure approximately 4" from the top of the background fabric, and mark a line with a washable marking pen.

- Place the top edge of the hanky on the marked line, and topstitch in position. If you are using lace or a doily, stitch raw edge with a small zigzag stitch (1.5 wide and .9 long).

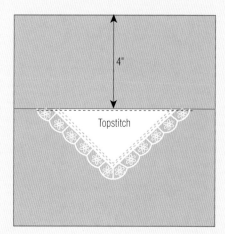

- Position the teacup appliqué over the top of the hanky. Press into position, following manufacturer's instructions for fusing. If you are using a no-sew fusible web, it's not necessary to stitch.

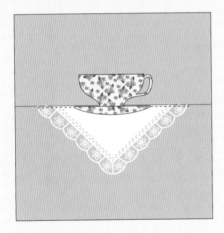

5. Complete the appliqué.

- Use a fine-tip permanent fabric marker to draw the saucer line just below the cup.

- If you prefer to stitch the appliqué into position, attach an Open-Toe Foot to your sewing machine. The large opening in the center of this foot allows you to see the appliqué as you are stitching, and stitches pass easily under the foot. Adjust your sewing machine for a satin stitch, following your manual. Place a layer of tear-away stabilizer behind the appliqué, and satin stitch around the appliqué.

6. Complete the wall hanging.

- Place the backing on your work area, wrong-side up. Place the batting on top of the backing. Place the appliquéd background on top of the batting, right-side up. Pin through all layers with curved basting pins to hold layers together. Echo quilt through all layers around the tea cup with a small straight stitch (stitch length = 2), if desired.

NOTABLE

It is impossible to stitch through some no-sew fusible webs. If you prefer to appliqué, use Steam-A-Seam 2 or a regular fusible web.

- Sew binding using your favorite method, or see page 14.

7. Attach grommets and ribbon for hanging.

- Insert grommets 1" and 1¾" from the edges on both sides of the wall hanging, following the package directions. Grommets should be just under the binding, at the top edge of the wall hanging.

- Thread a one-yard length of ribbon through each grommet. Bring all ends of ribbon together, and tie in a bow.

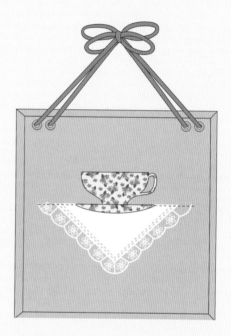

CHAI TEA MIX

20–22 SERVINGS

Chai (rhymes with "pie") is a spiced milk tea that has been around for centuries. Drinking chai is part of life in India. Chai is basically a rich black tea brewed with select spices, heavy milk and a sweetener. The most commonly used spices are ginger, cinnamon, cloves, cardamom, and pepper. The ingredients in chai are used to promote healing and strengthen various parts of the body. Indian chai has a warm soothing effect, acts as a natural digestive aid, and produces a wonderful sense of well-being. Chai it—you'll love this sweet, warm sensation!

This recipe is more "Americanized" than most, and seems to fit our fast-paced life style and taste preferences. The aromatic mixture is perfect to bag and give as a gift.

Ingredients:

1 cup powdered non-dairy creamer*

½ cup nonfat dry milk powder

1 tsp. vanilla powder

1 ¼ cups sugar

1 ¼ cups powdered unsweetened instant tea

½ tsp. ground cardamom

½ tsp. ground cloves

1 tsp. ground cinnamon

1 tsp. ground ginger

*I prefer Coffee-Mate.

Directions:

1. Combine ingredients in a bowl.

2. Process mixture in a blender until particles are fine and mixture is well blended.

3. Add two heaping tablespoons of Chai Tea Mix to an 8-ounce mug of hot water and stir well to mix.

For a chai milkshake, blend one cooled serving of chai with 2 cups vanilla ice cream. Delicious!

NOTABLE

If you can't find vanilla powder, mix one teaspoon of pure vanilla extract in with the sugar in the recipe until it is dry and well blended. Use a spoon or a mortar and pestle to combine the vanilla and sugar mixture.

Chapter 3:
A Frosty Glass —
Gifts with Class

Sip a frosty cooler as you make a gift with class. Or, put a batch of frosty slush in the freezer—it's like keeping a party "on ice" until you're ready for it!

BLOOMING FABRIC BASKET

FINISHED SIZE: FITS A SMALL TO MEDIUM BASKET

Use this technique to cover just about any size basket. It's a good way to salvage a favorite basket that is getting a little shabby. Coordinate colors for a party or your favorite holiday. Just add the blooms that will bring this lovely centerpiece to life!

Supplies:

½ yd. cotton fabric (Check cutting directions for figuring exact measurements)

1 pkg. polyester stuffing, 16 oz.

Hot glue gun or quick-drying glue*

Heavy thread, such as gimp or buttonhole twist

Matching all-purpose thread

8½" x 11" heavy cardboard

¼"–½" ribbon or trim to hide stitching line around basket rim. Measure around the rim and add 1" for overlap (optional)

1½" sheer wire-edged ribbon to cover handle. Measure length of handle, multiply by 1.5 and add 6" for over-hang on each side (optional)

½ yd. ½" wired ribbon for side ties (optional)

*I prefer Aleene's Thick Designer Tacky Glue.

Instructions:

1. Cut fabrics.

   • For the length, measure the depth of the basket and add 6".

   • For the width, measure the circumference of the basket. Multiply by 1.5 or 2, for full-ness. Cut one or more strips to equal this measurement when sewn together.

   • For the basket bottom, measure the diameter of widest part of the basket bottom and add 1".

Example: the basket depth measures 4". The length would be 4" plus 6" = 10". The circumfer-ence of the basket measures 21"; multiply by 2 = 42". Use one 10" crosswise strip of fabric for this basket top. For the basket bottom,

which measures 5" in diameter, another 6" (5" + 1" = 6") strip would be required. ½ yard of fabric was enough for this basket.

2. Prepare the basket bottom.

- Trace the basket bottom on heavy cardboard. Cut out just a little smaller than traced line.

- Cut a piece of fabric for the basket bottom about 1" larger on all edges than cardboard bottom. Baste around the fabric for the basket bottom with a heavy thread about ⅛" from the edge.

- Place the cardboard on the wrong side of the fabric that has been basted. Draw up the thread and fabric around the cardboard. When tight, tie thread ends together.

Circumference x 2

Depth + 6"

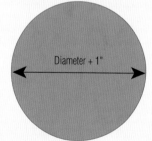

Diameter + 1"

Measure the basket to determine fabric yardage.

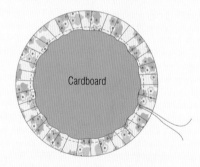

Cardboard

- Glue the fabric to the cardboard at gathers. Set aside.

3. Prepare the basket top.

- Sew the strip(s) for the basket top together to form a circle, right sides together. Use a ¼" seam allowance. Press down a 1½" hem on the top edge.

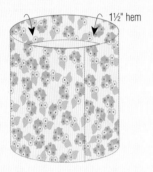

1½" hem

- Gather the top hem edge.
- Cut a length of heavy thread (such as gimp or buttonhole twist) the circumference of the basket top plus 10". Place a mark 5" from each end of the thread with a washable fabric marker. Quarter the top of fabric, and mark at each quarter. (Fold in half twice and mark.) Place one of the 5" marks on the thread at a quarter mark on the hem, pin

in place, and zigzag over the heavy thread at the inside edge of the hem. (Set zigzag width at about 4.0 and length at 2.0.) Pull up heavy thread to gather as you stitch.

Note: Be careful not to catch the heavy cord in the stitching. The zigzag stitch should just encase the cord.

- Overlap the 5" markings and tie in a knot.

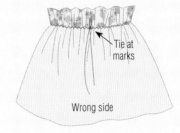

Tie at marks

Wrong side

- On the bottom edge of the fabric, zigzag over a piece of heavy thread that is about 10" longer than the piece used for the top of the basket. This thread is used to gather the bottom.

NOTABLE

The basket bottom is a great place to sign and date your creation!

NOTABLE

If you would like to add a second ruffle to the top edge of the basket, cut a strip of fabric that is the same width as the basket fabric, but only 2½" in length. Stitch the short edges together and fold in half. Gather the edge using heavy cord, the same as for the basket top. Glue this ruffled edge to the top of the basket before gluing the gathered basket cover to the basket.

• Even out the gathers at the top hem edge. Glue fabric to the top edge of the basket, leaving about 1" of hem extending above the rim of the basket.

4. Stuff the basket.

   • Turn the basket upside down and place stuffing inside the basket cover. The basket should look "puffy," but not overstuffed!

   • Pull the gathered thread at the fabric bottom over the bottom edge of the basket. Even the gathers, tie the gathering cord together, and glue to the basket bottom.

5. Complete the stuffed basket.

   • Glue the basket bottom that was set aside to the bottom of the basket, hiding the gathered fabric on the basket bottom.

   • Add trim (optional).

   • Wrap narrow ribbon or trim around the basket just under the fabric ruffle at the top of the basket. This trim will hide the stitching. Wrap the basket handle with the 1½" wire-edged ribbon, allowing the remaining ribbon to hang on the sides.

   • Cut the ½-yard length of ½" wire-edged ribbon in half. Tie a piece of the ½" ribbon on the bottom edge of each handle to secure the 1½" ribbon used to wrap the handle.

   • Trim with other ribbon as desired. Make a flower arrangement, or place a potted plant in the basket.

DOILY BLOSSOMS

Make a bouquet of beautiful blossoms to arrange in a fabric-covered basket or vase.

Supplies (for each blossom):

2 round Battenburg doilies, 4" wide

6"–9" length florist wire (vary the lengths of wire for each blossom if using in an arrangement)

Green florist tape

2 silk leaves, 1½" x 2"

1 bunch pearl head stamen

Instructions:

1. Create the blossom: Lay two doilies on top of one another with top petals in between each of the bottom petals.

Battenburg doilies

NOTABLE

If you would like to make the flowers without the wire, simply thread a needle, take a few stitches in the pinched flower edge and wrap with thread before tying off the thread end.

2. Complete the blossom:
   • Draw the wire from one bunch of stamen through the two doilies near the center. Pinch the bottom of the doilies together around the stamen to form a blossom.

• Add the first silk leaf about 1½" down the wire, and continue wrapping.

• Add another leaf on the opposite side of the wire about ½" from the first leaf.

Pinch doilies to form blossom.

Wrap stem with florist tape.

3. Create the stem.
   • Hold the wire from the stamen and the pinched blossom against a length of florist wire, and begin wrapping them with florist tape.

• Continue wrapping to the end of the wire. Trim excess tape.

Make several blossoms for an arrangement, or give a single blossom as a gift. These delicate flowers could also be made without the wire and stitched to a pin back or barrette.

ORANGE BLOSSOM FROSTINI
6–8 SERVINGS

This fruity drink will tickle your taste buds with a fresh Floridian flavor. Bouquets of lovely orange blossoms give way to the sweet, juicy oranges that make this drink so flavorful. Serve this slushy treat for a special summer brunch—orange juice is, after all, the quintessence of breakfast beverages!

Ingredients:

12 oz. can frozen orange juice concentrate

12 oz. gin

1 liter orange soda*

*I prefer Sunkist.

Directions:

1. Combine all ingredients. Stir until orange juice concentrate is melted.

2. Place the mixture in a container and freeze until slushy. Yes, it is that easy!

3. Serve Orange Blossom Frostini in a frosty glass dipped in sugar and garnished with an orange wedge and a sprig of mint. Add extra orange soda before serving, if desired. Spectacular!

For a treat fit for an island getaway, serve the Orange Blossom Frostini in a hollowed-out orange half with a short straw.

NOTABLE

For a frosty dipped glass, dip the rim of a glass in orange juice and then in sugar. Freeze until frosty.

ISLAND STAR WALL HANGING

FINISHED SIZE: 16" OCTAGON

Hand-dyed Balinese batik fabrics and an embroidered hibiscus flower give this star its tropical appearance. A folded three-dimensional star is a time-honored technique, revitalized with finesse for this easy-to-sew wall hanging. This project would also make a lovely table mat for your patio.

The hibiscus design is from John Deer's Adorable Ideas.

Supplies:

⅞ yd. Fabric A for center, backing and points

⅜ yd. Fabric B for points

⅜ yd. Fabric C for points

¾ yd. Fabric D for binding and points

6" gauge

Washable marker

Rotary cutter, mat, and ruler

9" x 11" sheet paper-backed fusible web*

Clear monofilament thread

Bobbin thread to match Fabric A

Embroidery design, rayon thread, lightweight bobbin thread, Hydro-stick stabilizer* (optional)

*I prefer Pellon Wonder-Under.

Instructions:

1. Cut fabrics.

   • From Fabric A:
   Cut one 16" square for the backing).
   Cut one 9" square for the center.
   Cut two 6" crosswise strips. Subcut into eight 6" squares for points.

   • From Fabric B (points):
   Cut two 6" crosswise strips. Subcut into eight 6" squares.

   • From Fabric C (points):
   Cut two 6" crosswise strips. Subcut into eight 6" squares.

   • From Fabric D:
   Cut two 2¼" crosswise strips for the binding.

NOTABLE

It is important to use a fusible web that can be stitched through easily.

- Cut three 6" crosswise strips. Subcut into sixteen 6" squares for points.

2. Press all 6" squares into prairie points (dimensional folded triangles).

   - Press 6" squares in half.

   - Press the folded ends to the center bottom, forming a sharp point exactly in the center.

3. Prepare the center and backing for embroidery (optional).

   - Find the center of the 9" and 16" squares by folding in half and pressing.

   - Press a 9" square of fusible web to the wrong side of the 9" fabric square, following manufacturer's directions.

   - Remove the paper backing on the 9" square, and center it in the middle of the 16" square, aligning center markings. Press into position.

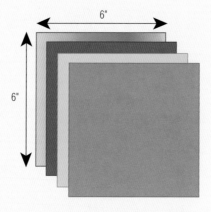

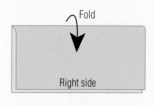

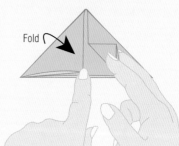

4. Mark the center lines, and mark diagonally from corner to corner with a washable fabric marker. It is important that these lines are accurate, because they will be used to line up the points of the star.

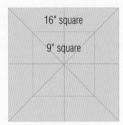

Mark centers.

5. Stitch the prairie points in position to form the Island Star.

- Place the first eight points on the marked lines 2" from the center to form the center star. Lift folded points and pin into position.

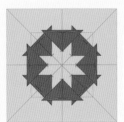

- Work with one folded point at a time, and lift the fold to stitch down the center from point to base.

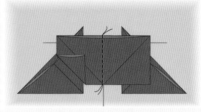

- Place the second group of eight points ⅝" from the tip of each of the first eight points. Pin and stitch as before.

- Place the third group of eight points ¾" from the tip of the second eight points. Pin and stitch as before.

NOTABLE

Complete machine embroidery after the star is stitched in position so that the markings don't become askew.

NOTABLE

Center a printed fabric design or use an appliqué instead of the embroidery.

• Place the fourth group of 16 points 4⅞" from the center. Position eight points on top of the previous row. Position the remaining eight points between each of the first eight points. All points should be an equal distance from the center.

Place remaining points.

6. Complete the wall hanging.

• Stitch around the outer edges to hold the last row of prairie points in position. Stitch in either a round or octagon shape.

• Prepare the binding.

• Cut one end of the binding on an angle. Press the binding in half lengthwise, wrong sides together. Attach binding around the outside edge of the wall hanging with a ¼" seam allowance, using your favorite method or following instructions on page 14.

• Prepare for machine embroidery (optional).

• Follow the general embroidery directions from your instruction manual.

• Place Hydro-stick stabilizer in an embroidery hoop, shiny-side up. Dampen the shiny side of the stabilizer with a sponge.

• Center and attach the wall hanging. Embroider the design, clip threads, and remove excess stabilizer.

If you don't have an embroidery machine, try using an appliquéd flower to complete the wall hanging!

PINA COLADA SLUSH

20–22 SERVINGS

You'd have to climb a coconut tree or bask in the sunshine under a palm to get more tropical "vibes" than a sip of this slushy creation will give you!

Ingredients:

16 oz. can cream of coconut paste

46 oz. can pineapple juice

3 cans (6 oz each.) frozen lemonade concentrate

3 cans (6 oz. each) water

2 cups light rum (optional)

Sour citrus soda*

Orange slices or pineapple chunks

Maraschino cherries

*I prefer Squirt.

Directions:

1. Mix all ingredients except the soda, orange, and cherries. Freeze.

2. To serve, scoop slush in a glass and add soda.

3. Garnish with an orange twist or chunk of pineapple and maraschino cherries.

Sip with a colorful straw, and turn your thoughts to a tropical island!

DOILY TREE ALBUM COVER

This holiday album cover is easy to make and a beautiful remembrance of a special year. The three-dimensional doily tree is reminiscent of a winter wonderland!

Supplies:

8½" x 11" top-loading photo album*

½ yd. cotton holiday fabric

⅓ yd. batting, enough for the front and back*

1 yd. of 1¼" lace (front cover only—double the amount for front and back covers)

2" x 4" rectangle polyester suede or felt for the tree base

Two 6" square cotton Battenburg doilies

Rotary mat, cutter, and ruler

Fabric glue,*

Spray adhesive*

Heavy water-soluble stabilizer*

Gold flat metallic thread*

Metallic needle, size 80/12

1 sheet poster board, 10" x 12" for the front inside cover

Small paint or stencil brush (optional)

½ yd. 1¼" lace for the tree bottom (optional)

Star button or ribbon rose and bow for the tree top (optional)

*I prefer the E-Z Load Memory Book, Pellon Thermolam Plus, Aleene's Thick Designer Tacky Glue, Sulky KK2000, Sulky Ultra Solvy, and Sulky Sliver Metallic thread.

Instructions:

1. Disassemble the album following directions given in album for page refills. Remove the screws, and remove the front and back cover. Keep the album pages together.

NOTABLE

An overspray box is nothing more than a cardboard box in which you place an item to spray with glue. It keeps the surrounding area from becoming sticky.

2. Cut the fabrics.
   - From the holiday fabric:
     - Cut one 13¼" x 13½" rectangle (album front).
     - Cut one 11" x 12¾" rectangle (album inside).
     - Cut one 2¼" x 11¾" rectangle (album binder area).
     - Cut one 9½" x 11⅜" rectangle from the batting.

3. Cover the album front with fabric.
   - Add a binding strip.
     - Fold under ¼" on short ends of album binding strip.
     - Place one long end just inside the binding edge of the album, and glue the strip in place. You will need to use an awl, punch, or other sharp object to open the screw holes on the fabric.

- Place the batting in an overspray box and spray with an adhesive spray. Affix the batting to the right side of the album cover.
- Place the fabric wrong-side up on your work area.
- Place the opened front album cover right-side down over fabric. The shorter measurement (13¼") is placed across the width of the album. One inch of fabric will extend on all sides of album except the binder side. ¾" of the fabric will extend on the binder side of the album.

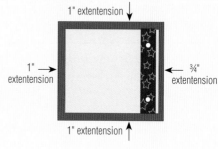

- Place a dab of glue in a dish or on wax paper. Use a small paint or stencil brush to glue fabric over corners of album and then sides, forming a miter at each corner.

Glue and miter corners; glue extensions.

4. Attach lace.

- Turn the beginning lace end under about ½", toward the wrong side, before gluing in place. Glue lace, right-side down, to inside album cover edges (except for the binding edge). Gather about ¾"–1" of lace at each corner to keep corners full and avoid a "pulled look."

Gather at corner.

- Turn the remaining lace edge under before gluing in place.

5. Cover the album inside front cover with fabric.

- Cut one 9½" x 11¼" piece of poster board to fit the inside cover.

- Place the 11" x 12¾" (album inside) fabric wrong-side up on work surface. Place the poster board on top of the fabric.

- Glue the corners in place, and then sides, mitering corners.

Cardboard

- Glue to the inside of the album, covering the edges of the lace.

Note: Repeat steps 2–5 to cover the album back, if desired.

6. Construct the doily tree using two 6" Battenburg doilies.

• Clip one doily apart at the corner loops so that there is one loop at the top and four on each side. Trim the inside of the doily, being careful not to cut through the Battenburg loops.

• Trim the inside of the remainder of the doily with one loop at the top and three on each side, being careful not to cut through the Battenburg loops.

• Clip the second doily apart so that there is one loop at top and two on each side. Trim the inside of this doily, being careful not to cut through the Battenburg loops.

• Take a small tuck on the upper inside edges of the larger doilies to ease out extra fullness and draw the doilies into a tree shape. Overlap the inside edges on the smallest trimmed doily to close up the center. Press the doily trees.

- Center the largest doily tree on a piece of heavyweight water-soluble stabilizer. Stitch or tack the pinned area into position through all thicknesses.

- Layer the second doily tree into position over the first, and stitch or tack. Follow with the third doily tree, and stitch or tack. Stitch through the center of all doilies, or tack at random, as desired, to secure the doilies together in a tree shape.

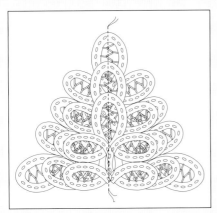

Heavy water-soluble stabilizer.

- Curve one or two 8" lengths of lace in an arc shape, and place them over the bottom edge of the tree (optional). Stitch at the top edge only.

- Clip excess water-soluble stabilizer from the back of the doilies. Spritz with a little water to remove remainder, if necessary.

7. Complete the tree base.

- Sandwich the 2" x 4" polyester suede rectangle between two layers of stabilizer.

NOTABLE
Shape cotton doilies by pressing them with a little steam.

- Stitch with a decorative stitch about ⅞" from one of the lengthwise edges, using a flat metallic thread.

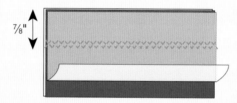

⅞"

- Clip off excess stabilizer.
- Copy and cut out the Tree Base below.

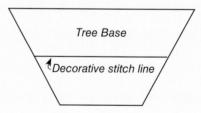

Tree Base

↑Decorative stitch line

- Use the pattern below to cut a Tree Base from the embellished suede, centering the decorative stitching line with the line on the pattern.

8. Add the tree to the album.

- Center the doily tree on the album front, and glue into position. Glue the tree base to the bottom of the tree.
- Glue a star button or small bow and ribbon rose at the top of the tree. Add crystals to the tree for extra sparkle.

Place holiday photos, mementos, or a holiday recipe collection in this precious keepsake! It will be treasured for years to come.

LIME FROSTY
24 FOUR-OZ. SERVINGS

Keep this frozen delight on hand over the holidays. It's the perfect festive drink for unexpected company. Joyfully refreshing any time of year!

Ingredients:

1 cup sugar

7 cups water

12 oz. can lemonade concentrate

12 oz. can orange juice concentrate

2 cups lime vodka

Green food coloring

*2 liters sour citrus soda**

Red and green maraschino cherries

Fresh lime

*I prefer 50/50 or Squirt.

Directions:

1. Cook sugar and water until sugar is dissolved.

2. Add lemonade and orange juice concentrate.

3. When mixture is cool, add lime vodka.

4. Add a few drops of green food coloring for a "holiday green" color.

5. To serve, place one large scoop of frosty mix in a glass and fill glass with citrus soda.

6. Garnish with red and green cherries and a slice of lime.

CANDLE COASTER

Quilt this lovely candle coaster without a sewing machine! The pieces are felted together like a puzzle. It's a fast and fun gift to give with your favorite scented candle.

Supplies:

10" square of black wool felt

9" x 12" piece of burgundy wool felt

9" x 12" piece of green wool felt

Felting needle mat and tool, or felting machine*

Temporary spray adhesive*

Metallic thread

Lightweight bobbin thread

Topstitching needle

*I prefer the Sewing With Nancy Fab Felter and Sulky KK2000.

Instructions:

1. Mark the vertical and horizontal center lines on a 12" square of paper. Position the Candle Coaster Backing pattern from page 155 four times, aligning the centers. Trace the outside lines only.

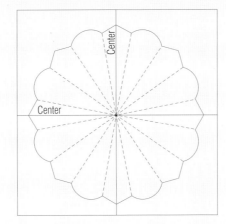

NOTABLE

Make sure your candle has a metallic or glass holder at the base to prevent melting wax damage to your coaster!

2. Cut out patterns from page 155.

   • Cut eight Rounded Top Petals from the burgundy wool felt.

   • Cut eight Triangle Top Petals from the green wool felt.

   • Cut one Backing from the black wool felt.

   • Cut one or two Center circles from the burgundy wool felt. Use a compass to draw circles 2¾" in diameter.

3. Spray the wrong side of the petals with a temporary spray adhesive in an overspray box. (Any cardboard box can be used for an overspray box to keep your workspace and project free from excess adhesive.)

4. Arrange the petals on the black background, alternating Rounded and Triangle Top Petals.

5. Felt the petals into position with the felting tool and mat. For more information about felting, see page 13.

6. Stitch a decorative stitch with metallic thread between each petal.

7. Position the center Circle, and felt in place.

Note: If you would like extra thickness in the center, place two circles on top of each other and felt together.

8. Add decorative machine stitching around the center with metallic thread.

FROSTY EGGNOG

6 SERVINGS

A variation of eggnog is served in just about every country in the world. It all started in England, where they used eggnog to toast to one's health. Rum is the liquor of choice in Puerto Rico, and the eggnog (coquito) is made with fresh coconut juice. Mexican eggnog, also known as rompope, features a heavy dose of Mexican cinnamon and rum.

This frosty American version of eggnog is a wonderful treat for Christmas morning when you finally get a chance to kick back and enjoy the spirit of the day.

Ingredients:

2 cups eggnog (regular or light)

1 tsp. nutmeg

½ cup vanilla ice cream

½ cup brandy (optional)

½ cup Amaretto liqueur (optional)

6 candy canes

Whipped topping

Freshly grated nutmeg or candy sprinkles

Directions:

1. Combine eggnog, nutmeg, ice cream, brandy, and Amaretto in a blender, and blend until smooth.

2. To serve: Pour eggnog into your favorite holiday glasses and garnish with a candy cane, whipped topping, and freshly grated nutmeg or colorful candy sprinkles.

NOTABLE

Make an easy candy garnish by placing hard candy in a plastic bag and using a mallet to break it into small pieces.

Chapter 4:
Some Like It Hot—
Heart Warming Gifts

Hot beverages have a way of making you feel cozy and comfortable, and these soothing drinks are no exception. No special holiday is required to serve warm refreshments, so cook up a new tradition!

HOMESPUN HOLIDAY GARLAND

SIZE: 40" GARLAND WITH 10" JUTE TIES AT EACH END FOR HANGING

Create a homespun garland to don your doorway at Christmas, or make the garland for another holiday by simply changing the decorations. It is a project that the whole family will enjoy making together!

Supplies:

⅛ yd. dark tan homespun fabric for the garland

Matching all-purpose thread

2 squares (9" each) of red and green homespun fabric for the ties

Pearls 'n Piping Foot

60" length of ³⁄₁₆" jute cording

⅛ yd. light tan homespun fabric for the gingermen

⅛ yd. red homespun fabric for the scrappy stars

2 pieces (4½" x 22" each) of cotton batting

Open Toe Foot

1 craft berry sprig with nine or more berry clusters

2 squares (4" each) cardstock

Temporary spray adhesive*

Water-soluble fabric marker

Fabric glue (optional)

*I prefer Sulky KK2000 spray adhesive.

Instructions:

1. Prepare the fabric.
   - Tear three 1¼" crosswise strips from the dark tan homespun fabric.
   - Cut four ½" x 9" green homespun fabric strips for ties and three ½" x 9" red homespun fabric strips for ties.
   - Cut the light tan homespun fabric for Gingermen in half to measure 4½" x 22" for each strip.
   - Cut the red homespun fabric for scrappy stars in half to measure 4½" x 22" for each strip.

2. Complete the Gingermen and Scrappy Stars.

- Trace or copy the Gingerman and Scrappy Star patterns from page 157. Glue or trace them on cardstock and cut them out.
- Layer one 4½" x 22" strip of light tan homespun fabric right-side down, one layer of cotton batting, and a second 4½" x 22" strip of light tan homespun fabric, right-side up. Spray each layer of fabric with temporary spray adhesive in a cardboard overspray box to hold layers together, if desired. (A simple cardboard box will keep the working area from becoming sticky.) Repeat, using the red homespun fabric.
- Spray the backs of Gingerman and Scrappy Star patterns with temporary spray adhesive in an overspray box.

• Place the Gingerman on the light tan fabric sandwich, and place a Scrappy Star on the red fabric at least 1" from the fabric edge. Stitch around outside edges of each pattern through all fabric layers with a short straight stitch length (2.0). Be careful not to stitch through the pattern.

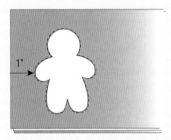

• Remove the patterns and reposition them about 1" from the first sewn pattern. Respray pattern pieces as necessary. Repeat the process until you have stitched three or more Gingermen and three or more Scrappy Stars.

• Trim the Gingermen and Scrappy Stars about ⅛"–¼" from the stitching through all layers.

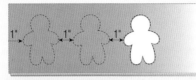

3. Complete the garland.

• Mark the jute cording with a water-soluble marker 10" from each end.

• Stitch the 1¼" dark tan homespun strips together with scant ¼" seam allowances, end to end. Press the seams open.

- Pin and stitch the 10" marking on the jute to the wrong side of the garland fabric near a short end.

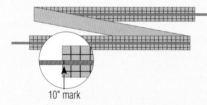

10" mark

- Set up your sewing machine with a long zigzag stitch (about 5.5 wide and 3.0 long), and attach the Pearls 'n Piping Foot.

- Zigzag stitch over the jute, pulling the jute in front of the foot to gather fabric behind the foot as you sew. When you have stitched to the opposite end of the garland, the remaining 10" mark should be even with the edge.

10" mark

- Twist the garland around the jute; stitch the jute to the edge of fabric to secure.

4. Decorate the garland.

- Evenly space and alternate the Gingermen and Scrappy Stars on the garland. Stitch in place by hand or glue in position with a fabric glue.

- Glue a berry cluster to the center (wrong side) of each of the seven ties. Allow the glue to dry, and evenly space ties between the Gingermen and Scrappy Stars, alternating colors. Tie the ties on the garland.

Decorations may twist on the garland. Make adjustments after hanging the garland.

CRANAPPLE CREEK WASSAIL
10–12 SERVINGS

This warm drink brings back pleasant memories of a simple life. As children, we played outside during the winter until our cheeks were rosy and our boots were full of snow. As we warmed ourselves by the fireplace, the holiday aroma of fresh-brewed wassail filled the kitchen. Create that special warmth in your own kitchen with wassail from the Dhein family homestead!

Ingredients:

48 oz. cranberry-apple juice

3 cups orange juice

¾ cup cinnamon syrup*

1 tsp. whole cloves tied in cheesecloth

Rum or wine to taste (optional)

Orange wedges and cinnamon sticks to garnish

*I prefer Savannah Cinnamon Mix.

Directions:

1. Tie the cloves in a 4" square of cheesecloth with heavy thread. Trim the excess cheesecloth close to the tie.

2. Combine all ingredients in a slow cooker. Simmer for several hours. The longer your wassail simmers, the more flavorful it will become!

3. Remove the cheesecloth bag of cloves when the flavor has reached its peak.

4. Add wine or rum, if desired.

5. Garnish with an orange wedge and a cinnamon stick stirrer.

SNOWFLOWER ORNAMENT

My father loved gardening and grew many beautiful flowers. In the winter when he longed to be outside working with his plants, he told us stories of enchanting snowflowers. When snowflakes stuck to our windows, we would look closely at them to find the ones that looked like his beloved snowflowers. You don't need snow flurries for these lovely ornaments, just felt and your sewing machine!

Supplies (for one Snowflower):

3 squares (5" each) of white felt or white glitter felt

Matching all-purpose thread

Sharp embroidery or appliqué scissors

Pinking shears

6" fine cord for hanger

Chenille needle with large eye

Fine-tip water-soluble fabric marker

Open Toe Foot

Light box

5" square water-soluble stabilizer*

Temporary spray adhesive*

20" of ⅞" sheer ribbon

White glitter glue

*I prefer Sulky Ultra Solvy stabilizer and Sulky KK2000 spray adhesive.

Instructions:

1. Mark the center line on paper. Position the Snowflower pattern, found on page 156, two times, aligning the centers. Trace. Repeat for the Backing pattern, found on page 156 in red.

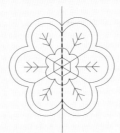

2. Cut the felt.
   - Cut two snowflowers from felt using the Snowflower pattern.
   - Cut one backing from felt using the Backing pattern.

3. Transfer the design to the right side of one Snowflower.

   • Place the paper design on a light box, right-side up.

   • Place the Snowflower over the design, right-side up, lining up the edges.

   • Trace the design on the felt Snowflower with a fabric marker.

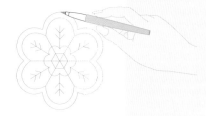

4. Stitch the designs on the Snow-flowers.

   • Place the two felt snowflowers together, right-side up, with the traced design on top.

   • Place a layer of water-soluble stabilizer between the two felt Snowflowers.

• Lightly spray-glue the layers together in an overspray box. A simple cardboard box will keep your working area from getting sticky.

• Stitch through all three layers, following the transferred design.

• Carefully trim close to the design stitching with a sharp pair of scissors, top layer only. Trim only the inner areas.

• Trim any excess stabilizer from the outside edges.

5. Gently wash out markings and remaining stabilizer by hand. Pat off excess water, and let the snowflower dry.

6. Attach felt backing piece and complete the snowflower.

- Center the stitched snowflowers on top of the right side of backing piece, and spray glue in position.

- Stitch over previous stitching ¼" from the snowflower edges. Go through all layers.

- Trim top layer close to the stitching line.

- Trim middle layer close to trimmed top layer with a pinking shears, and trim the backing layer about ¹⁄₁₆"–⅛" from the middle layer with a pinking shears.

- Sew cord hanger to top of snowflower using the large-eyed needle, and accent with a bow made of sheer ribbon, if desired.

- Brush the Snowflower lightly with glitter glue (optional).

Hang a beautiful snowflower in a window with a suction cup hanger, or make several to use as decorative coasters. They're a charming gift to give with a jar of yummy Hot Custard Mix!

NOTABLE

The scissors should glide on top of the water-soluble stabilizer, keeping you from cutting through the second layer of felt.

HOT CUSTARD MIX

12–14 SERVINGS

Sip this creamy hot custard delight as you cuddle up and read your favorite book in a comfy chair. Keep a decorative jar filled to the rim with custard mix so that it's easy to fix and enjoy at a moment's notice!

Ingredients:

4 cups instant nonfat dry milk powder

2 pkgs. (4 ½ oz. each) no-bake custard mix

1 ½ cups nondairy coffee creamer*

2 tsp. ground nutmeg

Whipped topping

Freshly grated nutmeg

Cinnamon sticks

*I prefer Coffee-mate.

Directions:

1. Combine all ingredients except the whipped topping, fresh nutmeg, and cinnamon sticks. Mix thoroughly.

2. Store in an airtight container.

3. To serve, stir ½ cup custard mix into an 8-oz. mug of hot water. Garnish with a dollop of whipped topping, sprinkles of freshly grated nutmeg, and a cinnamon stick.

For a cold, creamy treat, place 1 cup water and 1 cup custard mix in a blender. Blend until smooth. Add 1 cup of ice cubes, a few at a time, until blended and creamy.

NOTABLE

For freshly grated nutmeg, use a nutmeg grater or microplane. Gently rub the nutmeg over the grater surface. Sprinkle fresh nutmeg on whipped topping to garnish.

WINDOW MUG MAT

SIZE: 5¼" SQUARE

Pair up this novel mat with a ceramic mug for a great gift! Embroider the center of a mat in the spirit of a holiday for a unique flair.

Supplies:

9" square cotton print fabric

6" square lighter colored base fabric to embroider

8½" square Steam-A-Seam 2 no-sew paper-backed fusible web*

Compass

Washable fabric marker

Rotary cutter, mat, and ruler

Thread to match fabrics

Temporary spray adhesive*

9" square and 5¼" square batting*

Scalloping or pinking shears

Embroidery supplies: Embroidery design to fit in a 2" square, 9" square tear-away stabilizer, rayon embroidery thread, temporary adhesive spray, and embroidery scissors (optional)

*I prefer Sulky KK2000 spray adhesive and Pellon Thermolam Plus batting.

The leaf embroidery design is from The Amazing Designs Autumn Brilliance collection from Sewing With Nancy.

Instructions:

1. Prepare the circular mat back.

   • Remove one of the paper layers from the fusible web. Use the layer with the webbing attached for the project.

   • Center and fuse the 8½" square fusible web with webbing attached to the wrong side of the 9" square of print fabric, following manufacturer's instructions.

   • Mark an 8" circle on the paper side of the fusible web using a compass or an 8" luncheon plate. Cut out the circle with a scalloping shears. Cut directly on the line. Peel off the paper and set aside.

2. Prepare the base fabric for embroidery (optional).

   • Spray-glue a 9" square of stabilizer to the 9" batting square. Use a cardboard overspray box to keep the surrounding area from becoming sticky. Place the stabilized batting square in the embroidery hoop.

   • Trim the 6" square base fabric to a 5¼" square. Find the center of the square, and mark the vertical and horizontal center lines for embroidery, using a washable fabric marker. Spray-glue the wrong side of the 5¼" base square, and center the square on top of the batting in the hoop, lining up the center marks with the markings on the hoop.

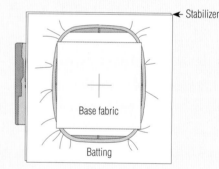

3. Embroider the base fabric (optional).

   • Set up your embroidery machine, following the manufacturer's instructions. Center and stitch the embroidery design of your choice.

- Press the design, right-side down, on a terrycloth towel after embroidery is complete. Remove excess stabilizer.

4. Complete the mug mat.

- Square up the batting and embroidered base fabric to 5¼". Spray glue and add the remaining piece of batting to the bottom of the embroidered base and batting section.

- Center the batting layers and embroidered design, right-side up, on the wrong side of the 8" scalloped circle.

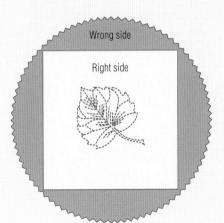

- Bring the ends of the circle up over the square on all four sides. Press to secure.

- Topstitch through all layers, stitching close to the scalloped edge.

NOTABLE

Make several mug mats for various holidays, with different fabrics and embroidery designs. Don't forget a birthday mat to give to a family member or co-worker for the special day!

WARM VIN BRULÉ

4–6 SERVINGS

In a quaint little village in Italy, people stand in their gardens on the first night of Epiphany, watching their bonfires blaze and drinking Vin Brulé to keep warm. You'll enjoy a warm feeling of contentment too, when you make this mulled wine to share with friends!

Ingredients:

1 bottle red table wine (substitute grape juice, if desired)*

1 lemon or orange peel studded with 3 or 4 cloves

⅛ tsp. grated nutmeg

Cinnamon sticks

½–1 cup sugar to taste

1 apple, peeled and cut in small chunks

Star fruit cut into star-shaped pieces

*I prefer Cabernet or Merlot wine.

Directions:

1. Pour the wine into a saucepan and bring to a boil.

2. Reduce heat to simmer, and add sugar slowly; stir to dissolve.

3. Add lemon peel or orange peel studded with cloves, nutmeg, one cinnamon stick, and apple chunks.

4. Simmer for 10–15 minutes. Remove the cirtus peel, cinnamon stick and apple chunks.

5. Serve in a clear glass mug or pottery wine glass with a cinnamon stick stirrer and a piece of star fruit.

NOTABLE

Thinly peel the lemon or orange so that there is no white pith on the peel, as this makes the wine taste bitter.

This spiced wine is a traditional Italian apértif, or a drink served before a meal. It's a wine that makes you feel warm all over!

APPLE DESSERT MAT

We serve Grandma's traditional German apple kuchen on these dessert-sized mats. Or, use them as mug mats for a large cup of Apple Cider Nog. It's a gift with taste!

Supplies (for two mats):

4 squares (10" each) red wool felt

8" square piece of green wool felt

Felting needle mat and felting needle tool, or felting machine*

Temporary spray adhesive*

Green all-purpose thread (optional)

*I prefer the Baby Lock Embellisher and Sulky KK2000.

Instructions:

1. Enlarge the Apple and Apple Base pattern on page 154 following instructions on page 12.

2. Cut out the pattern pieces.

   • Cut one leaf for each mat from the green felt using the Leaf pattern.

   • Cut two of the Apple Base patterns and two Apple patterns from the red felt.

   • Cut two stems from the tan felt using the Stem pattern.

NOTABLE

To make matching napkin rings, reduce the apple base pattern to measure 2" x 2". Reduce the apple, leaf, and stem proportionally. Felt or glue the apple pieces together. Glue or sew the apple to the center of a 9" length of ½" ribbon to tie on a napkin.

3. Complete the mats by felting them together.

• Spray the wrong side of the stems with temporary spray adhesive in an overspray box. Felt the stems into position on red apple bases with a felting tool and mat. For more information about the felting mat and tool, see page 13.

• Place red wool felt apples in position on the apple bases, covering tip of stems.

• Felt apples into position with the felting tool and mat.

• Spray wrong side of leaves with a temporary spray adhesive in an overspray box. Place a leaf on each apple where indicated.

• Felt the leaves into position with the felting tool and mat.

• Stitch veins in the leaves through all layers, if desired.

APPLE CIDER NOG

6 SERVINGS

In the fall when the air is brisk and leaves a myriad of color, the apples are ready to harvest. Apple cider is plentiful, and there is no comparison to the fresh, crisp taste. This recipe is a combination of our two family favorites—apple cider and eggnog! It's indescribably delicious!

Ingredients:

2 beaten eggs

½ cup sugar

1 cup apple cider or juice

¼ tsp. salt

¼ tsp. cinnamon

⅛ tsp. nutmeg

3 cups scalded milk

Whipped topping

Cinnamon sticks

Crushed red cinnamon candy

Directions:

1. Combine the eggs, sugar, cider, salt, and spices.

2. Scald the milk in a sauce pan. Do not boil!

3. Add the scalded milk gradually to the egg mixture, stirring constantly. Heat the mixture slowly in a saucepan.

4. Pour the hot Apple Cider Nog in mugs, and garnish with a dollop of whipped topping and crushed red cinnamon candy. Add a cinnamon stick to stir.

TORTILLA WARMER

Have you ever been frustrated using wax paper or paper towels to warm tortillas? The Tortilla Warmer is perfect to warm small or larger amounts of tortillas in your microwave in seconds!

Supplies:

½ yd. cotton print fabric

½ yd. muslin

½ yd. cotton batting*

Matching cotton thread

Yardstick compass and ruler or yardstick

Pinking shears

*I prefer Warm and Natural.

Instructions:

1. Prepare the pattern.

Note: Wash and dry fabric and batting according to manufacturer's instructions before making the Tortilla Warmer.

- Draw three 13" circles on paper using the yardstick compass.
- Use the circles drawn to complete patterns.

- Label one full circle "Top."

- On the second circle pattern, measure down 5" from the top and draw a line across the pattern at that point. Cut on line and label the 5" section "Flap." Mark a seam line ½" from the straight edge.

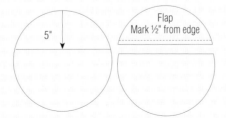

NOTABLE

The distance between the lead and the compass point should be half the amount (6½") of the complete circle.

• On the third circle pattern, measure up 11¼" from the bottom and draw a line across the pattern at that point. Cut on line and label the 11¼" section "Bottom." Mark a seam line ½" from the straight edge.

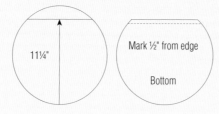

11¼"

Mark ½" from edge

Bottom

2. Cut one Top, one Flap, and one Bottom from the print fabric, muslin, and cotton batting. Trim ½" from muslin and batting Flap and Bottom at the straight edge.

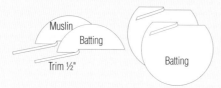

Muslin

Batting

Trim ½"

Batting

3. Prepare the Flap and Bottom.

• Serge or zigzag the straight edge of the print fabric Flap and Bottom to finish the edge.

• Layer the Flap: print fabric face-down, batting, and muslin right-side up.

• Layer the Bottom: print fabric face-down, batting, and muslin right-side up.

• Line up the curved edges of the Flaps. Repeat with the bottoms.

• Fold the finished edges of the print fabric over the muslin and batting, and pin in place. Stitch. Repeat with the bottom.

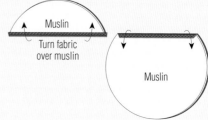

Muslin

Turn fabric over muslin

Muslin

4. Complete the Tortilla Warmer.

- Place the muslin Top on the work surface right-side down, then add the batting Top, and finally add the print fabric Top, right-side up.

- Position the Bottom over the Top layers with right sides of print fabric together and circular edges even.

- Position the Flap on the opposite end with the print fabric, right-side down.

- Pin through all layers to secure. Stitch around the circle with a ⅜" seam allowance. Remove pins and trim seam allowance with a pinking shears through all layers.

- Turn right-side out.

5. Lift bottom opening, place tortillas inside, and place Bottom side down in microwave. Microwave 10 seconds for one tortilla and 30 seconds to heat 4–6 at once. Microwave cooking times may vary. Test to see what works best for your microwave.

Please be responsible and never leave your microwave unattended when cooking. Follow your manufacturer's instructions to set cooking time.

NOTABLE

The Tortilla Warmer is machine washable. Dry slightly to remove any wrinkles, then hang to dry completely.

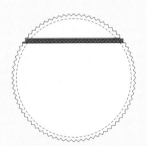

Stitch through all layers and trim with pinking shears.

MEXICAN HOT CHOCOLATE

1 SERVING

Come in from the cold after sledding or shoveling snow, and enjoy a cup of this hot, frothy delight. You'll be comforted by the warmth and the rich creamy essence of chocolate. Sip a cup as you work on your favorite project or relax in the comfort of your favorite chair.

Ingredients:

1 cup milk

½ tsp. vanilla, or seeds from one vanilla bean

1 oz. semi-sweet baking chocolate (or semi-sweet chocolate chips)

1 oz. milk chocolate bar or chips

1 cinnamon stick or ground cinnamon

Whipped topping

Directions:

1. Pour milk and vanilla, or vanilla bean seeds, into a one-quart saucepan on medium-high heat.

   Note: To remove the seeds from a vanilla bean, gently slit the bean through the top layer with a paring knife. Use the tip of a spoon to scrape the seeds from the bean.

2. Break the chocolate into pieces. Place the chocolate pieces in the saucepan with the milk. Stir constantly with a wooden spoon. Turn down the heat as the chocolate starts to melt, and stir until it is completely melted. Turn off the heat.

3. Whisk the chocolate milk with a whisk or Molinillo until foamy, about 30–60 seconds.

4. Pour into mugs, garnish with a dollop of whipped topping, and sprinkle with ground cinnamon. Place a cinnamon stick in the mug to stir. Enjoy!

NOTABLE

A Molinillo (moh-lee-NEE-yoh) is a wooden whisk used to froth hot chocolate. It is traditionally hand carved with designs burnt into the wood. Place the Molinillo in the hot chocolate and quickly rub the wooden handle back and forth in your palms to froth the chocolate. If you don't have a Molinillo, use a wire whisk with a wooden handle. It's not as authentic, but it works!

Chapter 5:
Classic Celebrations —
Luck, Laughter,
and Love

When the major holidays have passed, keep the joyous spirit alive! Add some handmade fun to the classic celebrations of spring and summer. Create many happy memories by living, laughing, and loving!

WOVEN FABRIC BASKET

Use these darling little baskets for a small plant or party favors. They're very creative and fun to make.

Supplies:

⅓ yd. cotton print fabric

9" x 15" no-sew paper-backed fusible web*

Rotary cutter, mat, and ruler

Fabric glue*

Small clip clothespins

1 yd. lace trim for edges of handle (optional)

Serger, clear serger foot, Fray Check, and 3 spools 12 wt. cotton thread to match fabric (optional)

*I prefer Steam-A-Seam 2 and Aleene's Designer Tacky Fabric Glue.

Instructions:

1. Cut and fuse the fabrics.

- Cut two 10" x 15" pieces cotton-print fabric.

- Cut one 9" x 14½" piece of no-sew fusible web.

- Center the paper-back sheet of fusible web on the wrong side of one of the 10" x 15" pieces cotton print fabric. Press according to manufacturer's instructions. Cool.

- Remove paper from fusible web and place the remaining piece of cotton print fabric over web. Fuse in position.

2. Cut fabric strips.

- Even off one of the 15" length-wise fabric edges by trimming off ⅜"–½".

- Cut the remaining fabric (starting at the trimmed side) into thirteen ⅝" x 15" strips. Twelve strips are used for weaving. and the thirteenth strip is used for the handle.

NOTABLE

If you are using 9" x 12" sheets of no-sew fusible web, you will need to slightly overlap a second 3" x 9" piece of fusible web for length.

NOTABLE

Don't worry about the fusible not extending to the edges of the fabric because the edges will be trimmed off later.

3. Weave fabric strips.

- Place six strips vertical on your work surface.

- Weave six strips over and under the vertical strips. Alternate each row, and center weaving. Push woven strips close together in center of the woven area. Woven area measures approximately 3¾" square.

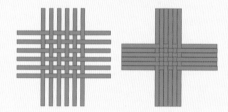

- Place a small amount of glue between the fabric strips close to the edges of the weaving.

- Press corners of strips as shown in the illustration, using three strips from each side.

- Start weaving at corners and continue up the sides. Clip strips together at the top edge with a small clothespin, if desired. Continue weaving with remaining strips until all four sides are woven. Basket should measure about 3¼" from the bottom edge to tip of points.

4. Complete the basket top.

- Bend down ends of the strips at the top of the basket to form points. Glue in position and trim off the excess strip.

- Glue trim on both lengthwise edges of the handle. Or, create serger lace.

5. Create serger lace for the basket handle, stitching three rows on each side (optional).

- Set up your serger for a 3-thread overlock, using the settings in your instruction manual.

- Thread the left needle and upper and lower loopers with 12 wt. cotton thread that coordinates with basket fabric.

- Stitch the first row on the basket handle using a wide stitch width and a stitch length of 3.

Note: Guide stitching on all rows by lining up the edge of the stitching with the right needle marking on the clear serger foot.

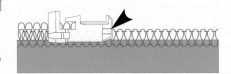

- Bring the needle to the highest position, raise presser foot, and flip the basket handle to the reverse side.

- Leave the stitch width at a wide setting for the next two rows, but shorten the stitch length to 2.

NOTABLE

With some sergers, you may need to place a strip of water-soluble stabilizer under the stitches when making serger lace.

- Stitch along the edge of the previous row, lining up edge of the stitching with the right needle mark on the clear serger foot. The shorter length setting adds more stitches, causing the lace to ruffle.

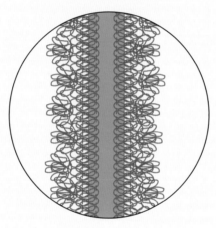

- Bring needle to the highest position, raise presser foot, and flip the basket handle back to the first side.

- Stitch along the edge of the second row, lining up the edge of the stitching with the right needle mark on the clear serger foot.

- Repeat directions for all three rows of stitching for the opposite side of the basket handle.

- Adjust handle length as desired by trimming. (The pictured handle is 10" long, allowing ½" to be turned under on each end.) Seal ends of thread with a seam sealant.

- Turn edge of handle under and topstitch before gluing into position (optional).

- Glue handle inside basket on opposite sides.

IRISH JOE COCKTAIL

1 SERVING

Celebrate St. Patrick's Day, even if you're not Irish. It's a day for "Wearin' of the Green," dancing a jig, laughing at Irish jokes, and having a "Blarney Bash."

We can't all color rivers green like the Chicago River on St. Patrick's Day, but the magic of turning an orange drink green seems quite Irish in the scheme of things.

Live a little!

Ingredients:

4 oz. orange juice

1–2 oz. Blue Curacao

Ice, as desired

Orange wedge

Directions:

1. Fill a glass with ice.

2. Pour orange juice over the ice.

3. Add Blue Curacao and stir until the cocktail turns a bright Irish green. It's like magic!

4. Garnish with a clover stir stick and orange wedge.

Dance a little jig and celebrate the luck of the Irish!

GRILL MASTER HAT

Surprise the chef with a hat and barbecue mitt. You'll probably be the first one served!

Supplies:

¾ yd. cotton Fabric A (crown of hat)

¼ yd. coordinating cotton Fabric B (hat band)

¼ yd. medium-weight to heavyweight iron-on interfacing*

1 yd. heavy thread, such as button-hole twist or gimp

Yardstick compass

Optional machine embroidery supplies: Design or lettering, rayon thread, lightweight bobbin thread, embroidery stabilizer, temporary basting spray, and curved embroidery scissors

*I prefer Pellon ShirTailor interfacing.

Instructions:

1. Make pattern for crown of the hat by drawing a 25" circle with the yardstick compass, following manufacturer's directions. (Distance from the point of the lead to the point of the compass should measure 12½".)

2. Cut fabrics.
   - Fabric A: Cut one 25" circle using pattern created for crown of hat.
   - Fabric B: Measure around top of head about ½" above ears. Add ½" to that measurement for seam allowances. Cut the fabric strip 8" x hat band measurement.

     Example: If your head measures 22½", add ½" seam allowance = hat band measurement. The strip would be cut 8" x 23".)
   - Interfacing: Cut strip the same measurement as hat band.

3. Fuse interfacing to the wrong side of the hat band following manufacturer's instructions.

4. Prepare for embroidery.
   - Fold band in half lengthwise. Press mark.
   - Fold band in half crosswise. Press mark.

★Grill Master★

- Center and mark embroidery placement on top half of band between seam allowance and lengthwise fold mark.

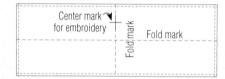

Center mark for embroidery

Fold mark

Fold mark

- Hoop stabilizer.
- Spray wrong side of hat band with temporary basting spray.
- Center the hat band, right-side up, in hoop. Embroider.

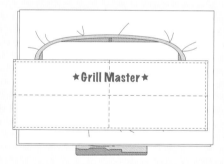

★Grill Master★

5. Stitch the short ends of the hat band, right sides together, using a ¼" seam allowance.

6. Gather the crown of the hat.
   - Cut a heavy thread about 20" longer than the head measurement.

     (Example: 22½" + 20" = 42½")
   - Place a mark on the heavy thread 10" from each end using a water-soluble fabric marker. Quarter and mark remaining thread.
   - Quarter and mark the crown.
   - Position the heavy thread close to the edge of the circle (crown).
   - Zigzag stitch over the heavy thread, being careful not to catch it in the stitching.

• Pull up the gathers until the two 10" end marks meet, and pin or tie ends. Even out gathers, matching quarter marks.

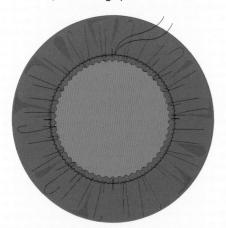

7. Attach crown to hat band.

  • Quarter mark hat band with a fabric marker.

  • Fold and press ¼" to the wrong side of the hat band on top edge.

• Stitch the lower edge of hat band to the crown with bottom right side of hat band to wrong side of crown, with raw edges even. Stitch from inside edge of crown.

• Fold the hat band in half, wrong sides together, along press mark. Topstitch band to right side of crown, covering gathers and previous stitching line. Stitch along folded edge of band.

NOTABLE

The hat band is easiest to stitch using a sewing machine with a free arm so that you are able to stitch from the right side of the hat.

BARBECUE MITT

Make a quick-to-sew Barbecue Mitt that is designed to grip utensils and pans with ease.

Supplies:

½ yd. cotton (print or solid) Fabric A

Matching all-purpose thread

⅓ yd. cotton Fabric B or muslin (lining)

⅓ yd. Quilted Iron Quick

⅓ yd. batting*

1 " Bias Tape Maker

*I prefer Pellon Thermolam Plus.

Instructions:

All seam allowances are ¼".

1. Enlarge patterns on page 120, following instructions on page 12.

2. Cut fabrics.

- Fabric A:
  - Cut one 8" x 10" rectangle.
  - Cut one 9" x 12" rectangle.
  - Cut one 1½" x 15" strip of bias.

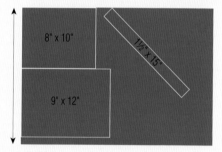

- Fabric B (lining):
  - Cut two 8" x 10" rectangles.
  - Cut one 9" x 12" rectangle.

- Quilted Iron Quick: Cut one 8" x 10" rectangle (right side is silver)

- Batting:
  - Cut two 8" x 10" rectangles.
  - Cut one 9" x 12" rectangle.

3. Layer and quilt fabrics.

- **Mitt Top**
  - Layer an 8" x 10" piece of Quilted Iron Quick (right-side down), batting, and Fabric B (right-side up).
  - Quilt layers together following the lines on the Quilted Iron Quick.
  - Cut one Mitt Top pattern from this quilted fabric.

- **Mitt Bottom**
  - Layer an 8" x 10" piece of Fabric A (right-side down), batting, and Fabric B (right-side up).
  - Quilt layers together with a free motion design or do a crisscross quilting design with lines 1" apart.
  - Cut one Mitt Bottom pattern from this quilted fabric.

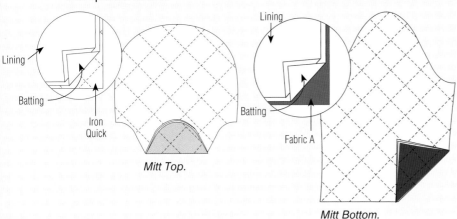

Mitt Top.

Mitt Bottom.

- Mitt Front
  - Layer a 9" x 12" piece of Fabric A (right-side down), batting, and Fabric B (right-side up).
  - Quilt layers together with a free-motion design, or do a crisscross quilting design with lines 1" apart.
  - Cut one Mitt Front pattern from this quilted fabric.

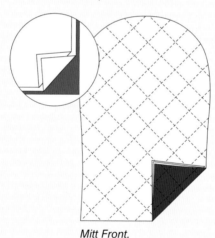

Mitt Front.

4. Complete mitt.

- Meet Mitt Top and Mitt Bottom, right sides together. Sew around thumb.

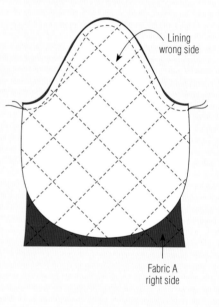

Lining wrong side

Fabric A right side

- Use a pinking shears to trim the seam.
- Fold thumb toward top of Mitt.
- Sew Mitt Front to Mitt Top/Bottom with right sides together; pink seam.

- Turn mitt right-side out. It looks small, but it's efficient and handy!
- Sew bias to bottom edge of mitt.
- Place the bias in Bias Tape Maker. Follow manufacturer's directions for use.

- After pressing bias, unfold one edge and stitch bias to bottom edge of mitt, right sides together, along the first press mark.
- Turn bias to wrong side of mitt and topstitch folded edge in place, finishing ends as desired.

Give yourself a HAND! You've completed a great new mitt that will protect you from burns at the grill or oven.

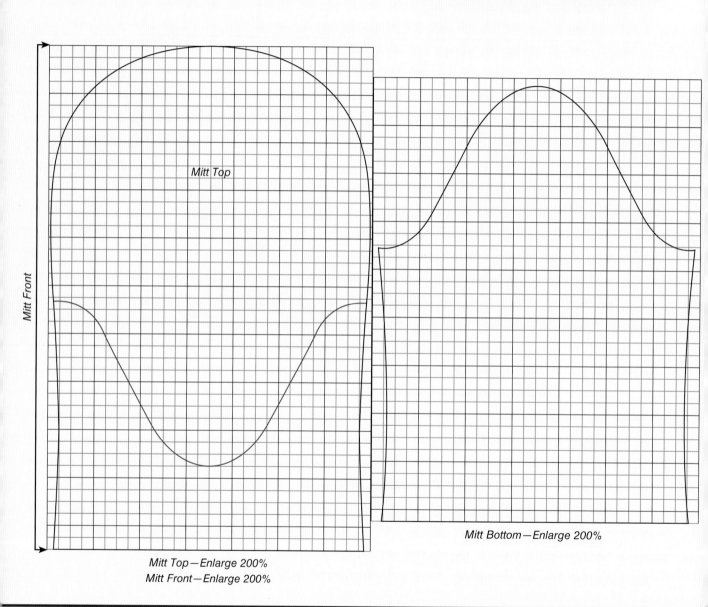

Mitt Front

Mitt Top

Mitt Top—Enlarge 200%
Mitt Front—Enlarge 200%

Mitt Bottom—Enlarge 200%

RASPBERRY LAFFY LEMONADE

6–8 SERVINGS

Lemonade is perfect for an outdoor barbecue, or any time you get together with friends and family for a little fun. Juicy red raspberries add the red to your red, white, and blue celebration. Have a perfect star-spangled picnic. Grill a little—and laugh a lot!

Ingredients:

Pre-sweetened raspberry lemonade mix, enough for a 2 qt. serving*

½ cup raspberry syrup*

1 cup raspberry juice*

7 cups water

Ice

2 slices lemon

½ cup fresh or frozen whole raspberries

*I prefer Country Time lemonade, Southern Raspberry Mix by Savannah Mixes, Inc., and Welch's Wild Raspberry Juice.

Directions:

1. Place raspberry lemonade mix in a 2 quart pitcher.

2. Add raspberry syrup, raspberry juice, and water. Stir.

3. Add ice, lemon slices, and raspberries. Stir.

4. Serve in tall glasses garnished with additional raspberries and a lemon slice.

STRING OF HEARTS

Show a little love when you give someone this String of Hearts wall hanging. If time is short, make one heart and insert a hanger, or add refrigerator magnets to the back. A simple gift with a whole lot of heart!

Supplies (for three hearts):

¼ yd. Fabric A (light-colored cotton for the front and back)

⅛ yd. Fabric B (cotton print for the heart top patches)

¼ yd. batting*

¾ yd. small braid trim or rick rack

1⅞ yd. ¼"–½" lace with a finished edge

¾ yd. ¼" satin ribbon

2 small plastic rings

Washable fabric marking pen

Temporary basting spray*

Magnets or 6½" wire hangers for single hearts (optional)

Machine embroidery supplies: Embroidery design, rayon thread, lightweight bobbin thread, tear-away stabilizer, and curved embroidery scissors (optional)

*I prefer Pellon Thermolam Plus and Sulky KK2000.

NOTABLE

The single heart refrigerator magnet in the photo was made by my 10-year-old granddaughter for her mom.

Instructions:

1. Cut fabrics.

   - Fabric A: Cut six 7" squares.
   - Fabric B: Cut six 3" x 4" strips.
   - Batting: Cut three 7" squares.

2. Cut trim, lace, and ribbon each into three pieces.

3. Create the heart pattern.

   - Trace or copy the Heart pattern from page 159 on paper. Cut out.
   - Mark a center line on paper.
   - Position the Heart pattern two times, aligning centers. Trace. (Include the center mark for embroidery, if desired.)

   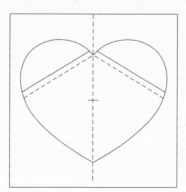

- Place three Fabric A squares on three batting squares.

- Pin the Heart pattern to each layered square, and cut out a heart.

- Fold back the paper heart pattern on the solid placement lines. Mark along the fold line on each side of the top hearts with a washable marking pen.

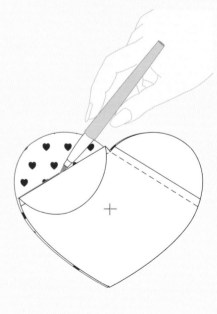

- Meet the 3" x 4" strips to Fabric A hearts, right sides together, with the 4" edge along the marked placement lines.

- Stitch a ¼" seam through all layers on each strip.

- Flip the strips up and finger press in place. Trim strips even with the top edge of the heart.

- Sew a small piece of braided trim over the seam lines on the heart front, if desired.

4. Prepare for embroidery (optional).

- Choose an embroidery design that will fit nicely on the heart(s).

- Transfer the center marking to each of the hearts that you plan to embroider for design placement.

- Hoop stabilizer.

- Spray the wrong side of your heart with temporary basting spray.

- Center the heart, right-side up, in your hoop. Embroider.

NOTABLE

If you are making single hearts, glue magnets to the back or stitch a hanger to the wrong side.

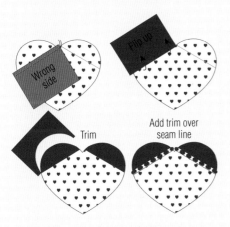

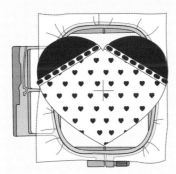

- Repeat for the remaining hearts. Remove excess stabilizer.

5. Finish the hearts.

- Place the hearts, right-side up, on the wrong side of the remaining Fabric A squares.
- Stitch around the outside edge of the heart through all layers with a small zigzag stitch.

Backing fabric wrong side

Zigzag around edges

- Trim the Fabric A backing square close to the stitching.
- Begin at the inner curve at the top of the hearts, and stitch lace to the outside edges on the right side of the hearts.
- Form bows with 9" lengths of satin ribbon. Stitch the bows to the hearts where the lace edges meet at the top inner curve.
- Tack the three hearts together by hand, or bartack by machine at the side edges.
- Stitch plastic rings to the top back of the end hearts to hang.

Attach rings to hang

STRAWBERRY VALENTINI

4–6 SERVINGS

Here's a perfect treat for Valentine's Day, but it doesn't have to be a special occasion. Make a special treat and give a little love anytime—your thoughtfulness will be appreciated.

Ingredients:

10 oz. sweetened frozen strawberries

6 oz. can frozen daiquiri mix

¾ cup light rum

3 cups ice

Chocolate-covered Strawberries:

1. Melt 6 oz. chocolate chips plus 1 tsp. shortening.

2. Dip 4-6 whole, fresh strawberries.

Directions:

1. Thaw frozen strawberries enough to cut into cubes.

2. Place strawberry cubes, daiquiri mix, and rum in blender; blend until mixed.

3. Add ice cubes a few at a time, and continue blending until slushy.

4. Pour into a plastic container; cover and freeze several hours or overnight.

5. Serve in a stemmed glass with a short straw and dessert spoon. Garnish with chocolate-covered strawberries and mint sprigs.

NOTABLE

Even the smallest amount of water on the strawberries when you dip them in chocolate can result in "seizing," when the chocolate becomes stiff and grainy.

Chapter 6:
Cool Concoctions and Crafts for Kids

The creamy concoctions in this chapter all have a smoothie or milk-shake consistency. They are blended with fruit and low-fat dairy products for vitamin and calcium-rich beverages with awesome taste. Children love to sip these nutritious soda shop treats, and they will also love the crafty gifts you create for them using the instructions provided. Enjoy!

SEASIDE SUNGLASS CASE

FINISHED SIZE: 4" X 7"

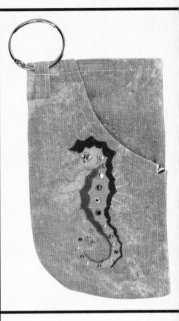

This clever case looks like a denim jeans pocket, but it holds sunglasses, sunblock, and pocket change. One Velcro closure pocket and one open jeans-type pocket makes it easy to stash your stuff. Attach the case to your jeans, beach tote, or bicycle with the easy clip ring.

Supplies:

¼ yd. cotton denim Fabric A (case)

¼ yd. cotton tropical-print Fabric B (case lining)

Matching all-purpose thread

Denim needle, size 16

1" ring clip

3" strip hook-and-loop tape

Embroidery supplies: Embroidery design, tear-away stabilizer*, rayon embroidery thread, lightweight bobbin thread, embroidery scissors, and crystals to embellish embroidery design (optional)

*I prefer Hydro-stick stabilizer.

Instructions:

All seams are ¼".

1. Enlarge and cut out sunglass case patterns on page 132, following instructions to enlarge on page 12.

2. Cut fabric.
   - Cut one Base pattern and one Pocket pattern from Fabric A.
   - Cut one Base pattern and one Pocket pattern from Fabric B.

3. Make belt loop.
   - Cut a piece of denim 1½" x 2".
   - Fold in half lengthwise and crease. Open and fold each edge to the crease. Fold in half. Edgestitch ⅛" from each edge.

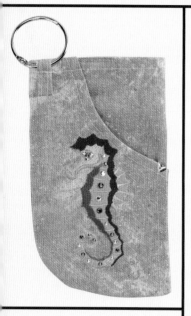

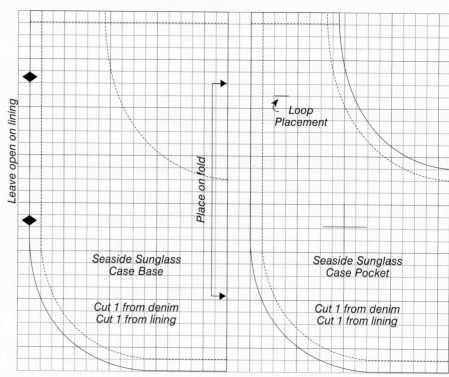

Leave open on lining

Place on fold

Loop
Placement

Seaside Sunglass
Case Base

Cut 1 from denim
Cut 1 from lining

Seaside Sunglass
Case Pocket

Cut 1 from denim
Cut 1 from lining

Base and pocket patterns measure 4¼" x 7½"—Enlarge 200%

- Pin belt loop to pocket section at mark indicated on pattern.

- Stitch, with right sides together, and flip up toward the top of case. Press. Baste in place.

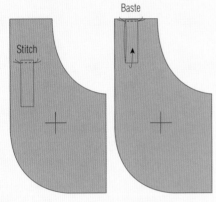

4. Embroider pocket section using mark on pattern to center design.

   - Hoop Hydro-stick stabilizer, shiny-side up.

   - Slightly dampen surface of stabilizer.

   - Attach denim pocket section, centering mark on pattern with center of embroidery hoop. Finger press into position.

- Embroider, following manufacturer's instructions.

- Remove excess stabilizer. Press from reverse side, if necessary.

5. Complete the pocket.

   - Place pocket and pocket lining sections right sides together. Stitch inside pocket curve and down side of pocket. Clip curve and trim corners. Press.

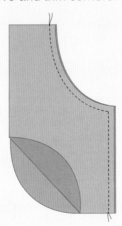

   - Turn lining to inside of pocket. Press into position with raw edges even.

   - Topstitch curve.

The Caribbean Seahorse embroidery design is from Embroidery Library and measures 1⅛" x 3¹³⁄₁₆"

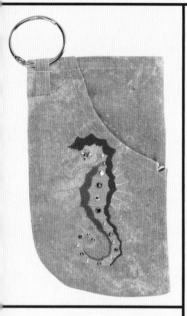

6. Complete case.

- Center pocket, right-side up, along fold line on left side of denim base. Baste top edges together. Topstitch close to side edge and ¼" away.

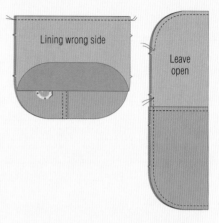

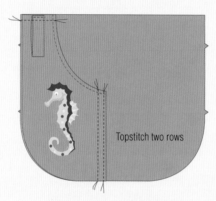

- Position the lining base over the denim pocket and base, right sides together. Stitch the top edge only. Press seam open.

- Fold the piece in half length-wise, and stitch around the lining and pocket, leaving an open space between the notches. Trim the corners.

- Turn the case right-side out through the opening.

- Stitch the opening between the notches shut by hand or machine.

- Tuck the lining inside the case.

- Stitch hook-and-loop tape in place inside the top edge of the case.

- Topstitch about ¼" from the top of the belt loop. Slide an open ring through top of belt loop and snap closed.

- Add colored crystals to embroidery design, if desired.

TROPICAL TUITI FRUITI

2–3 SERVINGS

This fruit smoothie is thick and delicious! Add a bit of wheat germ or protein powder for extra nutrition.

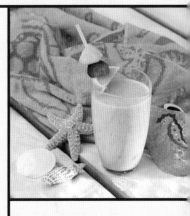

Ingredients:

15.25 oz. can tropical fruit

1 cup (8 oz.) mango or banana lowfat yogurt

½ tsp. banana or coconut extract

1–2 packets artificial sweetener or honey to taste (optional)

Ice or frozen banana (optional)

Fresh fruit skewer garnish (use fruits such as bananas, pineapple or orange wedges, cherries, melon, papaya chunks, and strawberries)

*I prefer Splenda artificial sweetener.

Directions:

1. Add tropical fruit, yogurt, and extract to blender.

2. Blend until smooth.

3. Add sweetener, if desired.

4. Blend until smooth.

5. Garnish with a fresh fruit skewer, and add a paper parasol—it's a mini "sunbrella!"

Mom and Dad love this Tuiti Fruiti smoothie, too!

NOTABLE

Add ice or frozen banana if you would like a slushier smoothie.

BAUBLE BOX

FINISHED SIZE: 4½" LONG X 4½" WIDE X 2¾" HIGH

This soft fabric box holds a child's trinkets and mementos. Personalize the box with embroidery, and give it with a gift card for an ice cream treat. It's a present that's sure to be cherished for years to come.

Supplies:

⅓ yd. cotton print fabric for box and box lining

1 button for closure

1 elastic pony tail holder for closure

Water-soluble fabric marker

Polyester fiberfil

6" square polyester batting*

Matching all-purpose thread

Machine embroidery supplies: Rayon thread, embroidery needle, lightweight bobbin thread, embroidery design or lettering, tear-away stabilizer, temporary basting spray, and curved embroidery scissors (optional)

2½" x 4" interfaced rectangle solid fabric for embroidery, ⅜ yd. each of two colors mini rick-rack trim, and monofilament thread (optional)

*I prefer Pellon Thermolam Plus batting.

Instructions:

1. Enlarge and cut out Bauble Box pattern on page 138 following instructions to enlarge on page 12.

2. Cut the fabric:
   • From the cotton print, cut one box and one box lining using the Box pattern.

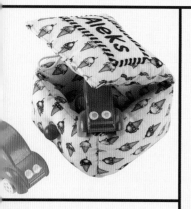

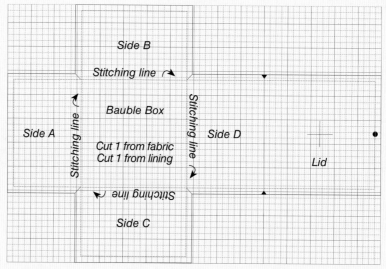

Bauble Box pattern measures 10¾" x 16" — Enlarge 400%

• Cut the batting into a 5" square for box lid. Baste batting to wrong side of box lid, ⅛" from the edge, and baste stitch an X from corner to corner.

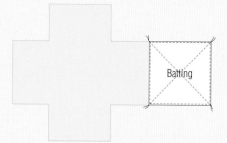

3. Embroider the box lid, if desired.

- Center and mark the embroidery placement on the box lid.

- Hoop the stabilizer.

- Spray the wrong side of the box lid with temporary basting spray.

- Center the box lid, right-side up, in your hoop. Embroider.

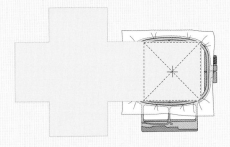

- Clip threads and press from reverse side, using a press cloth if necessary.

4. Stitch the lining to the box.

- Pin the lining to the box, right sides together.

- Stitch around the entire box, leaving the lid end open for turning.

- Clip the inside corners and trim the outer corners.

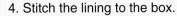

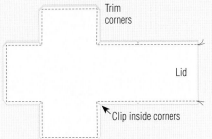

Trim corners

Lid

Clip inside corners

- Turn the box right-side out.

5. Stuff and stitch to complete the box.

- Mark stitching lines with a water-soluble fabric marker on the right side of the box.

NOTABLE

For a separate embroidery section as on photo, use a 2½" x 4" interfaced rectangle of solid fabric. Turn under and press all four edges after embroidery. Center and stitch to box lid. If desired, twist two lengths of rick rack together to trim edges. Stitch trim to box lid with monofilament thread.

The Lettering on box shown is the "Sponge" font from Designer's Gallery LetterWorks software, size 25 mm.

- Stuff Side A with polyfil, but not past the marked stitching line. Pin along the stitching line and stitch, sewing on the right side of the fabric. Repeat the stuffing and stitching directions for Sides B and C.
- Turn the box wrong-side out.
- Pin and stitch Sides A and B, right sides together, by hand. Take up a ⅛"–¼" seam through all four thicknesses. Repeat with Sides A and C.
- Turn the box right-side out.
- Stuff the box Bottom with polyfil. Pin and stitch on the marked line as before.
- Stuff Side D with polyfil. Pin and stitch.
- Turn the box wrong-side out, and stitch Sides C and D together, as with the other sides. Stitch the remaining Sides B and D together, and the box bottom will be complete.
- Position the lid squarely on the box, and stuff with polyfil.

- Pin and baste the elastic ponytail holder at the large dot, extending the holder past the seam to fit around the button you have chosen.
- Turn under lid and lining ¼" on the end of the box. The elastic holder extends to the outside of the lid. Stitch by hand to secure the opening. Topstitch, if desired.

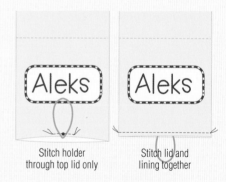

Stitch holder through top lid only

Stitch lid and lining together

- Sew button in place on box Side A, and place elastic holder over the button.

This chubby little Bauble Box is a real treasure!

CHOCONUT BANANA BUSTER

2–3 SERVINGS

This concoction looks like a soda shoppe treat, but it's nutritious enough for breakfast! It's a family favorite!

Ingredients:

1 cup milk

½ cup frozen lowfat yogurt

2 Tbsp. creamy peanut butter

1 large frozen banana, cut in chunks

½ tsp. banana extract

Maraschino cherries, chocolate syrup, and whipped cream

Chocolate-covered banana chunks (optional)

Note: Melt chocolate and dip bananas; then place in freezer until firm. Or, simply purchase chocolate-covered bananas in the freezer section at your supermarket.

Directions:

1. Place the first five ingredients in a blender.

2. Blend until smooth.

3. Drizzle chocolate syrup around the inside of a glass. Add the smoothie.

4. Garnish with a dollop of whipped cream, a cherry on top, and a skewer with a chunk of choco-late-covered banana.

NOTABLE

Place bananas that are getting a little too ripe in the freezer. Peel and cut them into chunks and place in a covered container. Label the container with contents and amount. They work great to thicken smoothies and add nutrition!

You don't have to be a child to enjoy this yummy smoothie. It is peanutty and chocolicious!

WAKE-UP WASH MITTS

FINISHED SIZE: APPROXIMATELY 8" X 9"

Babs the flop-eared bunny and Leo the lion will make your child's bath time playful! They start as washcloths, and end up as adorable puppet wash mitts. They're a dream to make—so easy!

Supplies:

2 washcloths for each mitt (gold washcloths for the lion and lavender for the flop-eared bunny)

Embroidery floss for facial features

Matching all-purpose thread

Water-soluble fabric marker

Darker all-purpose thread to stitch pattern outlines

3" square no-ravel fabric, such as Sensuede or washable felt, for each color appliqué: Lion—brown, black and tan. Bunny—black and pink.

6" square white polyester suede or washable felt for the bunny ears*

No-sew paper-backed fusible web*

Temporary spray adhesive*

Small pom pom for bunny nose

Medium-size pom pom for bunny tail (optional)

¼ yd. 1" gold polyester suede fringe for lion's mane

*I prefer Sensuede, Steam-A-Seam 2, and Sulky KK2000 spray adhesive.

Instructions:

1. Enlarge and cut out the pattern on page 158, following instructions for enlarging on page 12.

Enlarge and cut out the pattern on page 158, following instructions for enlarging on page 12.

NOTABLE

To make your own fringe, use a 1" x 9" strip of polyester suede or washable felt. Draw a line ¼" from one long end, and make clips ⅛" apart to meet the line along the strip.

NOTABLE

For the hand-embroidered backstitch, bring the needle up at 1, down at 2, and up again at 3. Go down at 1 and come up at 4 to continue stitching.

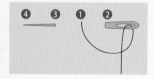

2. Transfer the pattern to a wash-cloth.

• Choose whichever pattern you are going to make.

• Lightly spray the wrong side of the Lion or Bunny pattern with temporary spray adhesive, and attach it to the right side of one washcloth, with the lower edge of the pattern along the finished edge (end with the woven band) of the washcloth.

• Baste around the pattern with dark thread to transfer the shape to the washcloth.

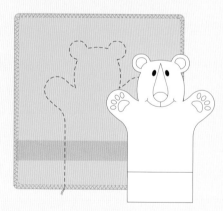

• Mark placement of appliqués and stitching detail before removing the pattern, if desired.

3. Add detail to the wash mitt.

• Trace the patterns for the appliqués from page 159 on the paper side of the fusible web. Follow the manufacturer's instructions. Trim the appliqués about ⅛" from the marked lines.

• Press the patterns to the wrong side of the polyester suede or washable felt, using a press cloth and a dry iron.

• Cut out the appliqués along the marked lines; remove paper backing.

• Position appliqués on wash mitt where indicated and press in place, using a press cloth and steam iron.

Lion details:

• Complete hand embroidery using three strands of floss. Use a backstitch for the mouth.

144

Bunny details:

- Complete the hand embroidery using three strands of floss. Use a straight stitch for the eyelashes and a backstitch for the mouth.
- Catch stitch a few pieces of floss or lightweight yarn for the bunny's whiskers, and stitch on a small pom pom for the nose.
- Complete the Bunny Ears.
  - Place the second washcloth and the suede or felt right sides together.
  - Spray glue the bunny ear patterns and place them on top of terrycloth and polyester suede or felt, right sides together, in the corner of the washcloth. Machine stitch close to patterns, leaving top open as far as the notch.

- Cut out bunny ears, leaving a ¼" seam allowance in open area. Seam allowance is NOT included in patterns. The remaining ear seam should be trimmed to about ⅛". Turn ears right-side out.
- Fold seam allowance in open area to the inside. Press. Topstitch around the ears closing the open area with the stitching.
- Position on bunny's head between dots, leaving ¼" extending past the pattern stitching line.
- Machine stitch ears to head on pattern line. Stitch ears into position.

NOTABLE

Place ears as far into corner of washcloth as possible to reserve room for wash mitt body.

NOTABLE

Place a small, wrapped bar of soap in the front pocket of the mitt. You've created a unique gift for a special child!

4. Complete the wash mitt

- Fold bottom edge of the appliquéd washcloth up 2¼", and topstitch the sides along the pattern line.

- Lay the second washcloth on work surface with right-side up.

- Lay appliquéd washcloth right side down on second washcloth, lining up folded edge with finished edge of second washcloth. Woven band on second wash cloth should be on top. Pin edges. (If you are making the bunny, make sure to pin the flop ears toward the center so that you don't catch them in the final stitching.)

- Stitch along pattern stitching lines, leaving bottom open.

- Cut out wash mitt trimming seam to ⅛". Clip curves and angles; trim corners.

- Turn right-side out.

Lion:

Stitch lion's mane to the back of the head through all layers with a zigzag stitch, using thread to match the washcloth. The stitches will blend into the terry cloth. Zigzag fringe, to back of lions head.

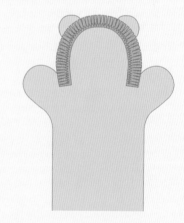

Bunny:

Stitch a medium pom pom to the bunny for a tail, if desired, stitching through the back layer of terrycloth only.

BANANA BERRY BOUNCE

2–3 SERVINGS

Wake up to this fruity smoothie for breakfast or make it for a quick pick-me-up. It's a good morning energizer!

Ingredients:

½ cup orange juice

2 frozen bananas (see page 141)

1 cup sliced strawberries, washed and hulled

2–3 Tbsp. honey (to taste)

Whole strawberries

Directions:

1. Place all ingredients except whole strawberries in a blender.

2. Blend until smooth.

3. Pour into glasses and garnish with a whole strawberry on each glass.

It's fresh and fruity!

NOTABLE

Add a tablespoon of wheat germ for an extra-nutritious smoothie!

SWEET DREAMS PILLOW COVER

FINISHED SIZE: APPROXIMATELY 16" X 20"

Your little child will adore this Sweet Dreams pillow! Make it for a special occasion such as "when the Tooth Fairy comes," as a throw pillow for the bed, or as a travel pillow. It will be a favorite naptime treasure!

Supplies:

½ yd. cotton fabric

Matching all-purpose thread

5" hook-and-loop tape

Water-soluble marker

Rotary cutter, mat, and ruler

12" x 16" pillow form

Instructions:

1. Cut the fabric: Cut a pillow cover 16½" x 43".

2. Clean finish each of the 16½"" edges of the fabric.
   - Press ½" to the wrong side.
   - Unfold and turn ¼" of the raw edge to the press mark.
   - Fold again on the the press mark, and stitch into position.

3. Complete the pillow cover.
   - Fold one of the finished edges toward the center of the cover, right sides together. (Fold in about 11".)

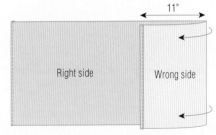

   - Overlap the finished edge from the opposite side, folding about 10¾" toward the center of the cover. There should be about a 1½" overlap.

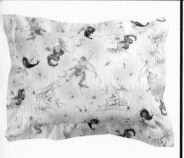

• Pin and stitch the side seams, using ¼" seams. Pink or serge the edges to finish them, if desired.

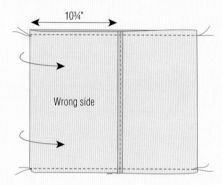

• Turn the pillow right-side out. Press.

• Measure and mark all sides of the pillow cover 2" from the edges. Stitch on the 2" marking to form the pillow flange.

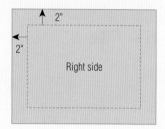

4. Add a hook-and-loop closure to the back overlap.

• Center and stitch the loop side of hook-and-loop tape to the under flap hem.

• Center and stitch hook side of hook-and-loop tape to the over flap hem.

5. Insert the pillow form.

A quick gift in a jiff!

CREAMY ORANGE DREAM
2–3 SERVINGS

This refreshing orange drink is like a creamsicle without the stick! A Creamy Orange Dream is a yummy treat for brunch or any time that you'd like a cool, energizing smoothie.

Ingredients:

⅓ cup frozen orange juice concentrate

½ cup milk

½ cup water

¼ cup sugar (or 4 pkg. artificial sweetener)

½ tsp. vanilla

5–6 ice cubes

Mint sprigs and orange wedges

Colorful straws

Directions:

1. Place the first six ingredients in a blender.

2. Blend until smooth.

3. Pour into glasses and serve with colorful straws. Garnish with mint sprigs and orange wedges.

It's cool and nutritious!

NOTABLE

Make a special box for when the Tooth Fairy comes! Use the Bauble Box instructions on page 137. Decrease the Bauble Box to measure 5" x 7⅛" for the Tooth Fairy box.

Resources

Barrett House
P.O. Box 540585
North Salt Lake, Utah 84054-0585
800-432-5776
www.Barrett-House.com
Wimpole Street Battenburg and lace

Clover Needlecraft, Inc.
13438 Alondra Blvd.
Cerritos, CA 90703 USA
800-233-1703
www.clover-usa.com
Felting Mat and Tool, sewing notions

Designs By Dhein
304 Fairway Dr.
Columbus, WI 53925
920-623-3727
designsbydhein.com

Duncan Enterprises
5673 E. Shields Ave.
Fresno, CA 93727
800-438-6226
www.aleenes.com
Aleene's glue

Embroidery Library, Inc.
16305 35th Avenue North #500
Plymouth, MN 55446
www.emblibrary.com
Embroidery designs online

John Deer's Adorable Ideas
1-866-492-DEER
www.adorableideas.com
Embroidery designs online

Libbey Inc.
300 Madison Ave.
P.O. Box 10060
Toledo, OH 43699-0060
www.libbey.com
Glassware

National Nonwovens
P.O. Box 150
Easthampton, MA 01027
www.nationalnonwovens.com
WoolFelt

Nancy's Notions
333 Beichl Ave.
Beaver Dam, WI 53916
1-800-833-0690
www.nancysnotions.com
Sewing, quilting, and embroidery supplies

Olfa North America
33 S. Sixth St.
Terre Haute, IN 47807
1-800-962-OLFA
www.olfa.com
Mats and cutters

Penzeys Spices
Brookfield, WI 53045
1-800-741-7787
www.penzeys.com
Spices, vanilla beans, cinnamon sticks

Prym Consumer USA, Inc.
P.O. Box 5028
Spartanburg, SC 29304
www.dritz.com
Omnigrid rulers, cutting mats, rotary cutters, other sewing notions

Savannah Cinnamon & Cookie Company
2604 Gregory St.
Savannah, GA 31404
www.savannahcinnamon.com
Savannah Cinnamon Mix and Raspberry Mix

Sew Precious Creations
www.sewpreciouscreations.com
Embroidery designs online

Sulky of America
980 Cobb Place Blvd. Suite 130
Kennesaw, GA 30144
1-800-874-4115
www.sulky.com
12 wt. cotton thread, KK2000 adhesive spray, stabilizers

The Warm Company
954 E. Union St.
Seattle, WA 98122
1-800-234-WARM
www.warmcompany.com
Steam-A-Seam 2, Warm & Natural batting

About the Author

Diane Dhein's love for cooking and sewing began in 4-H when she was 10 years old. The blue ribbons she earned at the county fair inspired her creativity in both the kitchen and the sewing room, and the Bachelor of Science degree in Home Economics (Family and Consumer Science) from the University of Wisconsin-Stevens Point was the springboard for her creative endeavors.

Diane has taught sewing-related classes throughout the United States and Canada for Nancy's Notions, where she was also the catalog fabric buyer, educational consultant, and retail store manager for 13 years. In addition to teaching high school home economics, she has owned a fabric store, designed patterns, was an education consultant for Baby Lock sewing machines, and was licensed as a Martha Pullen instructor. Diane's fond memories of 4-H have inspired her to become an accredited county fair judge.

She is currently employed as a technical writer at Nancy's Notions in Beaver Dam, Wisconsin, and has a small home-based business, "Designs by Dhein." Diane and her husband, Lynn, live near Madison, Wisconsin, and have two married daughters, one son, one grandson, and two granddaughters.

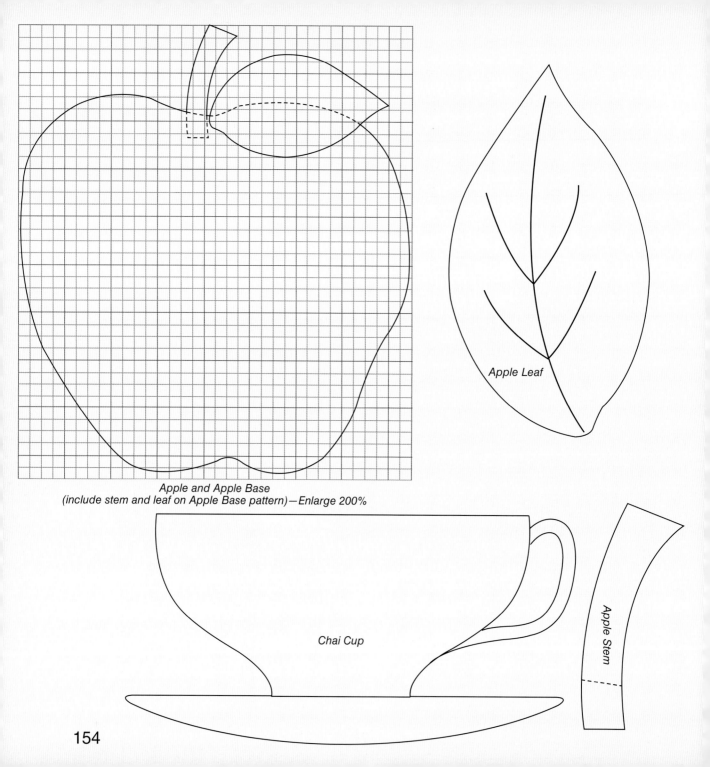

Apple and Apple Base
(include stem and leaf on Apple Base pattern)—Enlarge 200%

Apple Leaf

Chai Cup

Apple Stem

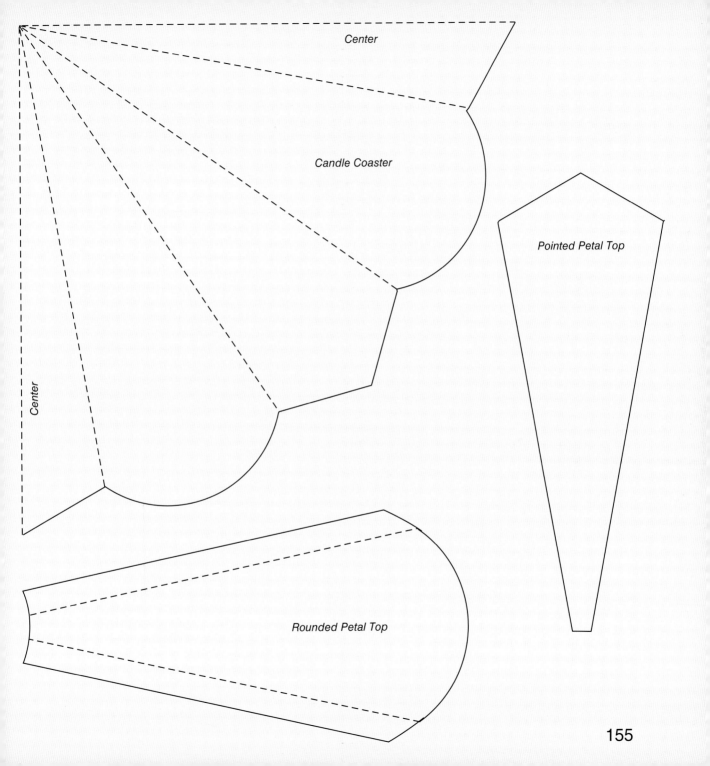

Center

Candle Coaster

Pointed Petal Top

Center

Rounded Petal Top

155

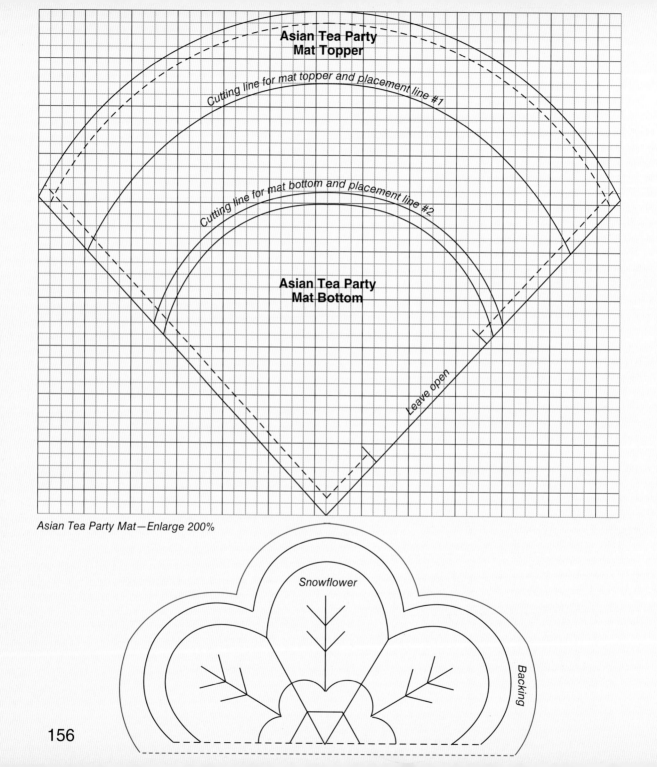

**Asian Tea Party
Mat Topper**

Cutting line for mat topper and placement line #1

Cutting line for mat bottom and placement line #2

**Asian Tea Party
Mat Bottom**

Leave open

Asian Tea Party Mat—Enlarge 200%

Snowflower

Backing

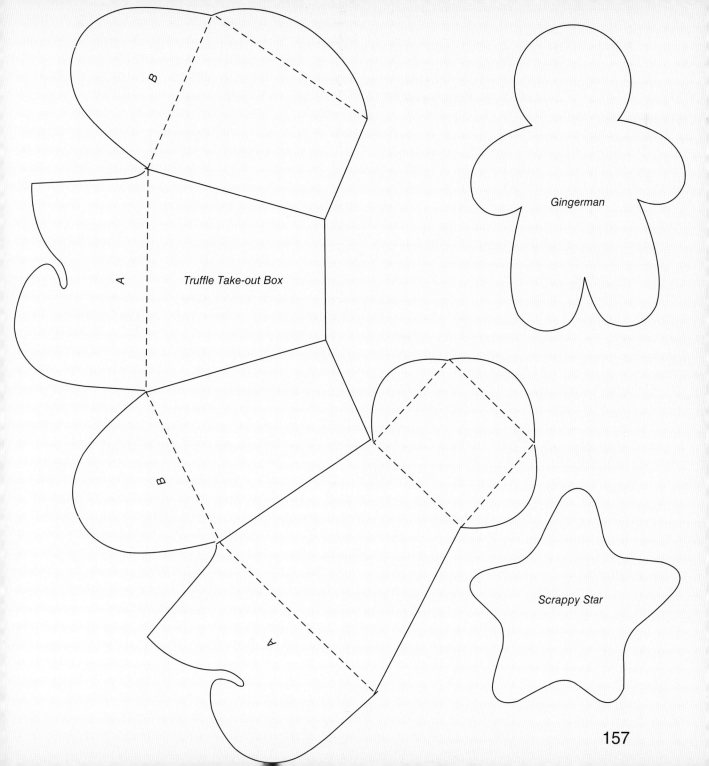

B

A

Truffle Take-out Box

B

A

Gingerman

Scrappy Star

157

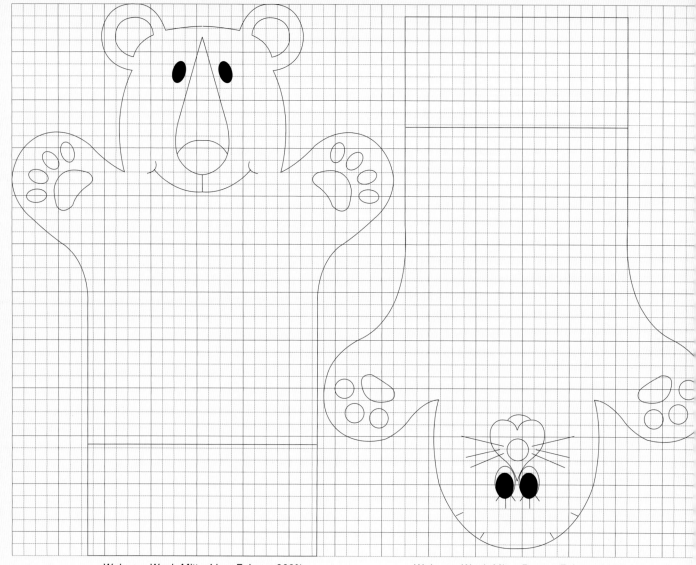

Wake-up Wash Mitt—Lion. Enlarge 200%   *Wake-up Wash Mitt—Bunny. Enlarge 200%*

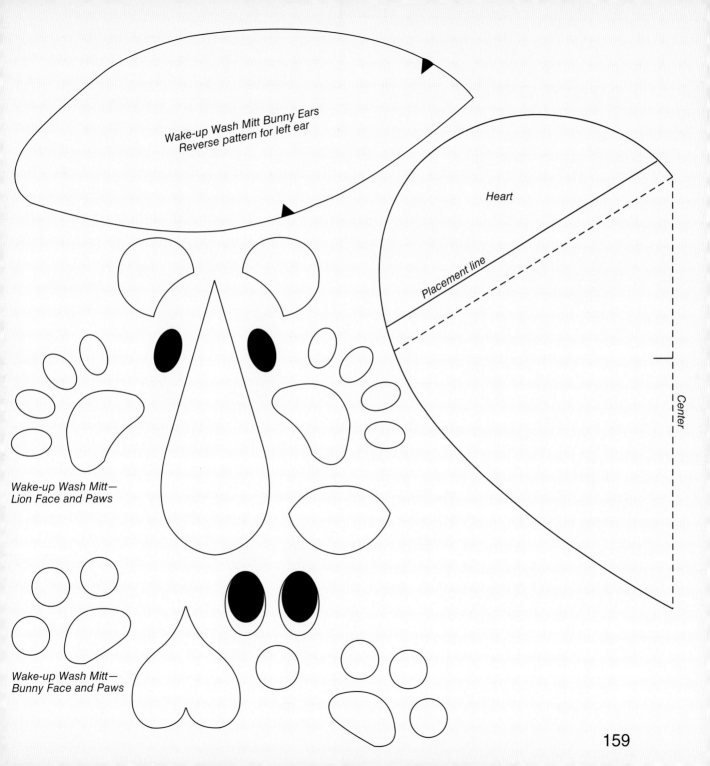

Wake-up Wash Mitt Bunny Ears
Reverse pattern for left ear

Heart

Placement line

Center

Wake-up Wash Mitt—
Lion Face and Paws

Wake-up Wash Mitt—
Bunny Face and Paws

Explore More Savvy Sewing Tips and Creative Combinations

Appli-Curves
Traditional Quilts with Easy No-Sew Curves
by Elaine Wald-schmitt

Learn the ins and outs of a new method for incorporating traditional curved pieced blocks including Drunkard's Path, New York Beauty and Hearts and Gizzards.

Softcover
8¼ x 10⅞ • 128 pages
200 color photos
Item# Z1659 • $24.99

Sew Easy as Pie
by Chris Malone

Explore flavorful chapters filled with creative cuisine ideas and delightful sewing designs, including Cherry appliquéd tea towels and Almond-Crust Cherry Pie, and an apple motif pot holder and Apple with Caramel pie.

Softcover
8 x 8 • 144 pages
50+ b&w photos
150 color photos
Item# Z0976 • $19.99

The Window Style Bible
500 Inspirational Ideas for Curtains, Blinds, Fabrics and Accessories
by Gina Moore

Big or small, contemporary or traditional, you're sure to find several stylish window projects that fit you and your budget, among the 500 ideas in this guide.

Softcover
8½ x 11 • 192 pages
500 color illus.
Item# Z1376 • $22.99

Kitchen Stitchin'
50 Quick and Easy Projects to Liven Up your Table
by Chris Malone

Quickly and easily create 50 distinctive pieces for kitchens and dining areas using quilting, embroidery, sewing, rug hooking, appliqué, beading and other techniques! This guide includes instructions for place mats, recipe album, toaster covers, napkins, wine bag, coasters and more.

Softcover
8¼ x 10⅞ • 128 pages
175+ color photos
Item# KTBLD • $21.99

No Sew, Low Sew Decorative Storage
50 Stylish Projects to Stash Your Stuff
by Carol Zentgraf & Elizabeth Dubicki

This collection of 50 inexpensive and easy-to-make storage solutions for the home can be completed with a hot glue gun, basic hand stitches, and other fast and easy techniques.

Softcover
8¼ x 10⅞ • 144 pages
100+ color photos
50 illus.
Item# DECST • $24.99